INSTANT KIWI

New Zealand in a nutshell

ROSEMARY HEPÖZDEN

NEW
HOLLAND

To my mother, Sylvia Grove McLernon,
the original instant Kiwi.

First published in 2014 by New Holland Publishers (NZ) Ltd
Auckland · Sydney · London · Cape Town

www.newhollandpublishers.co.nz

218 Lake Road, Northcote, Auckland 0627, New Zealand
Unit 1, 66 Gibbes Street, Chatswood, NSW 2067, Australia
The Chandlery, Unit 114, 50 Westminster Bridge Road, London, SE1 7QY, United Kingdom
Wembley Square, First Floor, Solan Road, Gardens, Cape Town 8001, South Africa

Publishing manager: Christine Thomson
Editor: Gillian Tewsley
Design: Kate Barraclough
Illustrations: Thomas Casey

National Library of New Zealand Cataloguing-in-Publication Data

Hepozden, Rosemary
Instant Kiwi : New Zealand in a nutshell / Rosemary Hepözden.
Includes bibliographical references and index.
ISBN 978-1-86966-409-1
1. New Zealand—Social life and customs. I. Title.
306.0993—dc 23

1 3 5 7 9 10 3 6 4 2

Printed in China by Toppan Leefung Printing Ltd, on paper sourced from sustainable forests.

Contents

Introduction

In 2013, a new record was set for the number of visitors to New Zealand. More than 2.7 million people – a 6 percent increase from the previous year – wanted to know what life is like in these small islands near the bottom of the world.

What makes people want to come here? What makes people want to stay? What makes people become Kiwi?

Our charms have not always been obvious. In 1909, Vladimir Ilyich Lenin described New Zealand as 'a country of inveterate, backwoods, thick-headed, egotistic philistines'. Clearly, it was not one of his better days. Over the last one hundred years, the rest of the world has discovered that Kiwis are friendly, laid-back and welcoming. Yes, we have our own quirky ways of doing things – a bit different, even from the Aussies – but our style and character (and even our accent) are quite endearing. We have mountains to ski down, hot mineral pools to bathe in, bridges to bungy off, and clean beaches to stroll along. We have our own, really cool airline. We are adventurous, creative, and bloody good at rugby. We split atoms. We climb the tallest peaks. We give women the vote before anybody else. We win Grammys at ridiculously young ages. We make movies that win loads of Oscars, and we grace royal tables with our fabulous world-class wines.

Yes, we're pretty proud of ourselves. But we don't always shout these things from the rooftop. Modesty, you see, is what makes us Kiwi. That's why Ed Hillary – the first man to conquer Mount Everest – became our most loved hero, when he reported to his mate : 'Well, George, we knocked the bastard off.'

Funny little place, New Zealand. This book begins to explain why.

Rosemary Hepözden

Chapter one

WHERE IN THE WORLD IS NEW ZEALAND?

Just where is New Zealand?

New Zealand, quite frankly, is all over the place. We could say it is:

- in the south-west Pacific Ocean
- located at the intersection of geographic coordinates 41°S and 174°E
- less than 500 kilometres from the International Date Line
- at the junction of the Pacific and the Australian tectonic plates
- 5430 kilometres from the South Pole (if a crow were flying it)
- on the opposite side of the world from Salamanca, Spain
- a 3-hour flight from Sydney, Australia
- between New Caledonia and Nicaragua in the index of an atlas
- at number 76 on a list of the world's countries ranked by total area
- at the lower left-hand end of the Pacific Ring of Fire.

But more important than all of these is that New Zealand is:

- at the centre of the universe, as far as we're concerned!

It's probably easiest to say that New Zealand is a small country south-east of Australia, comprising three main islands (the North Island, the South Island and Stewart Island) and some offshore islands. The largest of these other islands are the Chathams, about 870 kilometres east of Christchurch – far enough away that they have a separate time zone, 45 minutes ahead of the rest of New Zealand.

If you stretched a tape measure down the country in a gentle curve from the northern tip of the North Island to the southernmost point on Stewart Island, the distance would be slightly more than 1600 kilometres. We have somewhere between 15,000 kilometres and 18,000 kilometres of coastline; nobody can be exactly sure, because it wriggles in and out so much through headlands and harbours, inlets and estuaries.

LOCAL KNOWLEDGE

Time travel

Some people think New Zealand is an impossibly long way from the rest of the world. But if Captain Cook could manage the journey in the *Endeavour*, who can complain about the time it takes, especially with the benefit of 21st-century aircraft?

How far is Auckland from other large cities, and how long does it take to get there?

Sydney	2156km (1340 miles)	3h 00m
Tokyo	8840km (5493 miles)	10h 55m
Hong Kong	9140km (5679 miles)	11h 30m
Los Angeles	10,497km (6523 miles)	12h 15m
Shanghai	9383km (5830 miles)	12h 30m
Cape Town	11,763km (7310 miles)	17h 35m
New York	14,194km (8820 miles)	19h 25m
Rio de Janeiro	12,268km (7623 miles)	23h 30m
London	18,337km (11,394 miles)	24h 45m
Istanbul	17,041km (10,589 miles)	25h 20m
Rome	18,396km (11,431 miles)	28h 15m

The flight times might tempt you to think New Zealand must surely be at the bottom of the world. Nope. The closest bit of land to the South Pole is the southern tip of South America, so New Zealand can hardly be called the last place on earth.

How did New Zealand get here?

Well, it depends who you ask. Scientists reckon that New Zealand fractured off from the supercontinent Gondwanaland about 85 million years ago. The sea that flooded into the rift between the breakaway bit and the land mass left behind became the Tasman Sea. This explanation is credible, but it's painfully slow moving, a bit thin on detail, and not something you'd want to watch in real time.

The Māori have a much more action-packed legend. The details of this story vary according to who's telling it, but the punchline remains the same.

A good day's fishing

Māui was the youngest of five brothers. As he grew, he had so many hair-raising adventures – acquiring fire, holding back the sun, that sort of thing – that his brothers felt a bit uneasy in his company, and they certainly didn't want him joining their fishing expedition. Māui, however, had other ideas.

One day, he hid in the hull of his brothers' canoe, clutching a hook he had fashioned from a fragment of his grandmother's jawbone. Soon his brothers set sail, unaware of the stowaway on board. Only when they were far out to sea did Māui emerge from his hiding place. He urged them to sail even further, well out of sight of land.

Once the brothers began fishing, the bottom of their canoe was quickly filled with the catch. Then Māui decided his moment had arrived. When his brothers refused to give him any bait, he whacked himself on the nose to produce blood to smear on his magic hook. He threw the hook over the side of the canoe, chanting some powerful prayers as he did so.

Almost immediately, he snared something huge that struggled and lunged on the end of his line. Māui was worried what the sea god Tangaroa would think about his huge catch, and told his brothers that he would go and seek forgiveness from the gods for landing it. He warned his brothers to stay away from the fish until his return.

But his brothers got tired of waiting and began cutting pieces off the fish. The fish started to raise its fins and thrash around in agony as its flesh was mutilated. Soon the sun rose and, in the blazing heat, the fish solidified and became land, and the scars that Māui's brothers had carved into it became valleys and mountains. 'Te-Ika-a-Māui' ('the fish of Māui') is what we now know as the North Island.

What did you say the name was?

Kiwis are known for their informal and casual approach to things, so perhaps it shouldn't have come as a surprise when, in 2009, the New Zealand Geographic Board discovered that the names 'North Island' and 'South Island' – the rather unimaginative creations of European whalers – had never been adopted in law, even though they had been in use for more than 200 years. Just as baffling was the mysterious omission of the Māori names for the two islands, Te-Ika-a-Māui and Te Waipounamu ('the waters of greenstone'), from maps drawn after the 1950s. The Geographic Board decided to canvass public opinion on what to do.

Well! Opinions varied a great deal. Some thought it would be too confusing to juggle alternatives. Some loved the simplicity of 'North Island' and 'South Island'. Some said those names were 'somewhat bloody obvious'. Some said Māori names would be an enchanting and useful point of difference in tourism publicity. Others described the New Zealand Geographic Board as 'cultural zealots' and the move towards new names as political correctness of the worst kind.

In the end, in a rather typically Kiwi way, we decided to keep the fuss to a minimum. The Board formalised the English names for the North and South Islands, and assigned the Māori names Te-Ika-a-Māui and Te Waipounamu as official alternatives – thereby keeping everybody happy.

Aotearoa: a cloud on the horizon

If you listen carefully to the Māori version of our national anthem, at the end of the first verse you will hear another name for New Zealand: Aotearoa.

Mythology tells us that as the great voyager Kupe sailed across the South Pacific Ocean, his wife Hineteaparangi scanned the horizon for sign of land. When she called out 'He ao! He ao!' ('A cloud! A cloud!'), Kupe realised they were finally getting somewhere, because when you're at sea the appearance of a cloud often indicates the presence of land.

The North Island (and eventually the whole of New Zealand) became known as 'Aotearoa'. Not everybody agrees on the exact meaning of the word, but the most popular interpretation is 'long white cloud', referring to Kupe's discovery so long ago.

Where did the name 'New Zealand' come from?

The first European to sight New Zealand was the Dutch explorer Abel Tasman. He arrived in 1642 and called the country 'Staten Landt', but three years later Dutch mapmakers changed the name to 'Nova Zeelandia' after the Dutch province of Zeeland. The British explorer James Cook anglicised the name to 'New Zealand'.

More and more national organisations and businesses are now proudly incorporating both the Māori and English names in their title; for example, the Green Party of Aotearoa New Zealand, and the Human Rights Lawyers Association Aotearoa New Zealand.

Godzone: the divine favourite

Of course, we've also got a nickname for our country.

In the late 19th century, Irish-born poet Thomas Bracken recorded his love for his adopted homeland of New Zealand in a long and stirring poem called 'God's Own Country'. His enthusiasm was clearly contagious, because Richard ('King Dick') Seddon, the prime minister of the time, frequently used the phrase in his speeches and correspondence. The last time he used it was in a telegram composed on 10 June 1906, just before he departed Australia by ship for New Zealand: 'JUST LEAVING FOR GOD'S OWN COUNTRY'. Sadly, this turned out to be a case of famous last words, because Seddon died suddenly before he reached home.

Eventually, of course, some wit couldn't resist condensing the phrase 'God's own country' to 'Godzone', and it's been our nickname ever since.

Sizing us up: little and large

In rare moments of insecurity, if we start to feel a bit insignificant compared with North America or Europe, we can reassure ourselves that our country is *huge* compared with lots of other places. For example, New Zealand is:

- 6.5 times bigger than Switzerland
- 245 times bigger than Hong Kong
- 381 times bigger than Singapore
- 45,089 times bigger than Gibraltar
- 113,928 times bigger than Monaco
- 541,068 times bigger than the Vatican City.

The truth, though, is that New Zealand *is* petite when compared with:

- Kazakhstan, which is 10 times bigger
- India, which is 12 times bigger
- Australia, which is 28 times bigger
- China, which is 35 times bigger
- the US, which is 36 times bigger, and
- the Russian Federation, which is 63 times bigger than New Zealand.

New Zealand is a little bit bigger than the UK, and a bit smaller than Italy.

LOCAL KNOWLEDGE

Here are some placenames you won't find on the map.

across the Ditch	The 'Ditch' is the Tasman Sea, so to go 'across the Ditch' means to go to Australia
the Antipodes	Refers to New Zealand and Australia as on the opposite side of the world from Great Britain and Europe. (The geographical 'antipodes' of somewhere is the point on the Earth's surface that is diametrically opposite it)
the Basin	The Basin Reserve, a historical cricket ground in Wellington
Bay Cities	The 'Twin Cities' of Hastings and Napier, in Hawke's Bay
the Cake Tin	Wellington's Westpac Stadium, a venue for rugby matches
Central	Central Otago
City of Sails	Auckland
Cow Town	Hamilton
Down Under	A colloquial term for New Zealand (or Australia, or both of us together)
Dunners	Dunedin; also known as 'Edinburgh of the South'
Far North	The northern part of Northland, at the top of the North Island
Far South	The southernmost part of the South Island
the Garden City	Christchurch

Hibiscus Coast	A stretch of coast on the Hauraki Gulf from Whangaparaoa up to Waiwera
the House of Pain	Carisbrook, a Dunedin venue used for cricket and rugby matches since 1886, also called 'the Brook'; it was eventually dismantled in 2012
K Road	Karangahape Road in Auckland, a former red-light district now being upgraded with art galleries, cafés and clothing stores
the Mainland	The South Island
the Naki	The province of Taranaki
North Cape to the Bluff	From one end of New Zealand to the other
Palmy	An affectionate nickname for Palmerston North
Rotovegas	The nickname for Rotorua, because of the number of motels and neon lights
Remmers	Remuera, an affluent suburb of Auckland
the Shaky Isles	New Zealand, a nickname that refers to the frequent seismic activity here
The Middle of Middle-earth	Wellington, ever since the 2012 world premiere of *The Hobbit: An Unexpected Journey*
West Island	A cheeky nickname for Australia
Windy City	Wellington, also known as the 'City of Gales'
the Wrap	The province of Wairarapa

Chapter two

WHO ARE THE NEW ZEALANDERS?

Ethnic allsorts

When the 2013 Census came out, it revealed that we're getting more diverse and interesting all the time. It found out that a quarter of New Zealanders were born overseas, mainly in England, China and India. As a whole, we are:

European	74%
Māori	14.9%
Pacific peoples	7.4%
Asian	11.8%
Middle Eastern,	
Latin American, African	1.2%
Other ethnicity	1.7%

(The percentages add to more than 100 percent because some people identified with more than one ethnic group.)

The arrival of the Māori

Until about 800 years ago, Aotearoa was empty of human beings. But at the same time, as the Renaissance was about to get under way in Europe, the ancestors of today's Māori found their way to these shores.

These Polynesians were brilliant navigators, and would explore seemingly limitless areas of the South Pacific Ocean in waka (canoes). They could find their way out across the ocean thanks to observation, seamanship and an understanding of the natural world. Fixing their direction using the sun and stars, they had several methods for determining where land lay. They would follow the flight of migrating birds, for instance, knowing those birds would eventually land somewhere to feed. They looked for cloud formations created as air currents rose over mountains. And they knew that changes in the ocean's wave patterns – which they could pick up as vibrations when they lay in the hull of their canoe – were probably caused by a landmass in the vicinity. Once they had sighted new land and settled there, they were able to journey back home to tell friends and family about where they'd been and to encourage colonisation of the new land.

For a long time, people accepted the idea of a 'Great Fleet' – that Māori had migrated here together in a fleet of seven canoes – but anthropologists now think that they arrived at different times from around AD 1250 onwards.

The arrival of the Europeans

Four hundred years passed before European explorers discovered New Zealand – and initial contact made with the Māori population was far from promising.

Abel Janszoon Tasman, an employee of the Dutch East India Company, sailed eastwards from Australia and sighted the mountains of the west coast of the South Island on 13 December 1642. A few days later, near Farewell Spit at the top of the South Island, the first contact between Māori and European occurred. It didn't go well. On 19 December 1642, two Māori canoes paddled out to inspect Tasman's two ships. When Māori issued a challenging blast on long wooden trumpets, the Dutch responded on instruments of their own. What was intended as a cordial return greeting was interpreted by Māori as a willingness to fight.

When hostilities erupted and the body count mounted, Tasman decided to leave without placing foot on New Zealand soil, noting later that it was unrealistic to ever expect to surmount such cultural differences between the two peoples.

English navigator Captain James Cook fared better. He reached New Zealand on the *Endeavour* in October 1769. He charted the coastline and wrote a great deal about the place, and there was, for the most part, a mutual respect between him and the Māori he encountered. Despite a disastrous encounter during one of his voyages, when ten men under his command were killed and eaten by Māori, Cook was still able to describe the indigenous New Zealanders as having 'a brave, noble, open and benevolent disposition'.

But without an effective advertising campaign to tell people that paradise was waiting on the other side of the world, no more than a couple of hundred settlers had followed in Cook's footsteps, even 50 years later. These were, for the most part, whalers and sealers, traders in timber and flax, and a few earnest missionaries. Everybody else who pondered moving down here came to the conclusion that the distance was too great, the conditions too hard, and the rewards too few.

Waves of migration

Things changed with the signing of the Treaty of Waitangi in 1840. With a British colony now declared established, a commercial operation called the New Zealand Company was set up in London to boost numbers to the new settlement, and land was sold in 100-acre lots as the company's agents promoted a liberating lifestyle change. The dream on offer was something of a fantasy – some of the land sold had never been properly purchased from the Māori, much of the land had to be cleared before it could be used, and there was a general shortage of food – putting the new colony at risk of petering out before it ever got established.

The discovery of gold in the South Island in the 1860s brought a rush of Australians, Chinese, Americans, Scandinavians and other Europeans such as Dalmatians, Greeks and Italians. For the first time, the Māori population was outnumbered by arrivals from overseas. But the most active period of immigration was the 1870s, thanks in part to the increased efforts of the British Government and (somewhat fanciful) descriptions like that published in the *Labourers Union Chronicle*, for example, of New Zealand as a 'land of oil, olives and honey . . . the promised land for you'.

By the mid-1870s, the non-Māori population had risen to over 250,000, but migration stalled again until after World War II.

In the 1950s, realising that more people were needed to make the country a viable proposition, the government provided financial incentives to new migrants. More than 76,000 British came here as assisted immigrants; so, too, did 20,000 Dutch. In the mid-1950s, the first Asian students arrived from Malaysia, Thailand and Indonesia, and in the 1960s, around 50,000 labourers came here from Pacific islands such as Samoa, the Cook Islands, Niue and Tokelau. A wave of Tongan and Fijian Indian migration followed in the 1980s, as well as refugee groups from Laos, Cambodia and Vietnam. From 1987, a new scheme selected suitable immigrants on the basis of qualifications and the amount of capital they had to invest, attracting a large number of migrants from Taiwan, China and Hong Kong, as well as from South Africa.

Who are the New Zealanders?

Back in 1951, over 85 percent of foreign-born residents of New Zealand came from either Australia or the UK. Within 60 years, however, we have transformed ourselves from 'British backwater' to 'vigorously multicultural', with an expanded sense of identity and heritage.

These days, if you ask the question 'Who are the New Zealanders?' the answer has to be 'Anybody and everybody'. Projections prepared for the Ministry of Social Development show that while the 'European or Other' population will continue to form the largest group of New Zealanders (around 70 percent), over the next few years the Asian population is projected to have the largest relative growth: by 2025, it is reckoned, there will be as many people identifying as 'Asian' as those identifying as 'Māori'. Not surprisingly, the number of people who identify with more than one ethnic group is increasing, particularly among younger age groups.

All present and accounted for? New Zealanders overseas

Kiwis love to travel, and some like it so much they forget to come back. At last count, there were well over half a million Kiwis – about 648,000 – living across the Ditch. Britain has lured around 58,000 of us, and North America (Canada and the US) is currently home to about 32,000. Around 40,000 others are *somewhere* out there in the world.

Now you can be a New Zealander

Until 2006, the Census of Population and Dwellings always asked residents of New Zealand to describe themselves as either 'European', 'Māori', 'Asian', 'Pacific peoples' or 'Other'. This sometimes made things a bit awkward – why would you describe yourself as 'European' if several generations of your ancestors had been born in New Zealand? And why would you want to differentiate yourself as 'Māori' as opposed to 'Pākehā' (non-Māori) when we are supposed to be 'one people'? What if you were a bit of a mixture? We needed a new answer to the question of ethnic ID. The census taken on 7 March 2006 obliged: for the first time, people could identify themselves as 'New Zealander', pure and simple. The idea appealed to nearly 430,000 people (11.1 percent of the population) who took part in the 2006 Census. We finally seemed to know who we were and, from now on, would make no bones about it.

LOCAL KNOWLEDGE

A trans-Tasman truth

One of our favourite jokes was told by former prime minister Rob Muldoon in the 1980s. When asked if he was worried about the increasing exodus of Kiwis to our larger neighbour, he commented that anyone who left New Zealand to live in Australia was raising the average IQ of both countries. (Actually he pinched the line from the American Will Rogers, but we didn't mind one bit: anything that puts us in a favourable light compared with our neighbours is funny.)

Kiwi at heart or by heritage?

KIWI BY HERITAGE

Australians, we reckon, must feel a bit hard done by when it comes to local heroes – how else to explain their bold-faced attempts to poach some of ours, including this sample gang of seven?

Nancy Wake	The audacious World War II spy and saboteur codenamed 'the White Mouse', at one time placed at the top of the Gestapo's 'Most Wanted' list
Fact	Nancy was born in Wellington in 1912
Phar Lap	The magnificent racehorse. Okay, so his reputation was built up over there by winning 37 out of the 51 races he entered, including the 1930 Melbourne Cup, but you can't ignore his origins
Fact	Phar Lap was foaled in Timaru in 1926
Keith Urban	The Grammy Award-winning country singer and *American Idol* judge, married to leading Australian actress Nicole Kidman
Fact	Keith was born in Whangarei and lived there for the first two years of his life

Split Enz   The internationally beloved pop/rock group formed by Te Awamutu boys Tim and Neil Finn

Fact   Just before they toured Australia in 1973, they changed the band's name from 'Split Ends' to 'Split Enz', just so their Kiwi roots could never be overlooked

---

Russell Crowe   Our local lad turned Oscar-winning gladiator

Fact   Maybe he left the country at the age of four, but the boy was born in Wellington and his departure was not permanent. He later went to Auckland Grammar School

---

John Clarke   These days he may be making the Aussies laugh, but he was born in Palmerston North and came to fame by playing the laconic Kiwi farmer Fred Dagg

Fact   Kiwi as!

And the final word on this subject must go to:

Pavlova   No, definitely not Australian, according to the *Oxford English Dictionary*, which in its online edition launched in December 2010 pointed out that the recipe for this culinary icon was introduced to the world in *Davis Dainty Dishes*, published in 1927 by Kiwi company Davis Gelatine

KIWI AT HEART

Because we believe in the notion of a level playing field, we have to admit we're not totally averse to doing a bit of pinching ourselves. If you check their birth certificates, there are definitely one or two notable people we claim as Kiwis who were, in fact, born offshore. Okay, so they got their start somewhere else, but it took New Zealand to bring out their greatness . . .

Anna Paquin	The *True Blood* actress (and, we must mention, the second youngest Oscar winner ever for her supporting role in *The Piano*) was born in Winnipeg, Manitoba, Canada
Beatrice Tinsley	The astronomer and cosmologist who studied the evolution of galaxies and who, many think, was in line for a Nobel prize before her death at the age of just 40, was born in Chester, England
Derek Handley	The technology entrepreneur, aspiring astronaut and CEO of the B Team (set up by Sir Richard Branson to encourage businesses to 'prioritise people and planet alongside profit') was born in Hong Kong
Eleanor Catton	The youngest ever writer to win the prestigious Man Booker Prize for Fiction was born in London, Ontario, Canada
Irene van Dyk	The most capped international netballer of all time was born in Vereeniging, South Africa

Lydia Ko	The teenage golf sensation, who turned pro at the age of 16, was born in Seoul, South Korea
Marti Friedlander	One of New Zealand's favourite photographers, who brilliantly documented the 1981 anti-apartheid protests in New Zealand, was raised in a Jewish orphanage in London, England
Michael Joseph Savage	The first Labour prime minister of New Zealand and architect of the welfare state was born in Tatong, Victoria, Australia
Roger Donaldson	The film director, producer and writer whose successes include *Smash Palace* and *Dante's Peak* was born in Ballarat, Australia
Roger Hall	The hugely successful playwright behind *Glide Time* and *Middle Age Spread* was born in Essex, England
Sam Neill	The movie actor with a list of film appearances as long as your arm was born in Omagh, County Tyrone, Northern Ireland
The Wizard of New Zealand	Well loved for his oratory delivered from atop a ladder in Cathedral Square, Christchurch, the Wizard (aka Ian Brackenbury Channell) was born in London, England

Chapter three

MĀORI - AOTEAROA'S TANGATA WHENUA

The Treaty of Waitangi: it all starts here

On 6 February 1840, the Treaty of Waitangi was signed at Waitangi in the Bay of Islands by Captain William Hobson, several other English residents, and about 40 Māori chiefs. There were two texts, one Māori and one English, and some inexact translation produced different understandings of the agreement reached. The main thrust of the Treaty, however, was that Māori gave the Crown the right to establish a British colony, while the Crown guaranteed Māori full protection of their interests and status, and full citizenship rights.

The Waitangi Tribunal was established in 1975. It is a permanent commission of inquiry that responds to claims brought by Māori that promises made by the Crown in the Treaty of Waitangi have not been upheld.
See: www.waitangi-tribunal.govt.nz

The marae: standing on sacred ground

A 'marae' is a Māori communal facility with a meeting house, dining hall and cooking area. It symbolises the iwi (tribe) to whom it belongs. Although marae are communal, they are anything but a casual drop-in centre: all manuhiri (visitors) must be invited by a member of the tangata whenua (the owners of the marae). Because it is a sacred place, various rituals are followed. Before visiting, it would be wise to brush up on your marae etiquette.

The Beginner's Guide to Visiting the Marae is a useful documentary that can be found on the NZ On Screen website. It was made in 1984 – which means we must excuse the slight apprehension of the Pākehā visitor back then – but, says NZ On Screen, 'the doco remains an effective primer for 21st century marae novices'. You can watch it in two parts at:

www.nzonscreen.com/title/the-beginners-guide-to-visiting-the-marae-1984

How to do a hongi

If you visit a marae and one of your Māori hosts leans towards you, they're not expecting a kiss. They want you to share in a 'hongi', which is the traditional Māori greeting. Lean forward slightly, close your eyes, and let your nose press lightly against the nose of the other person – either directly on, or just to the side. It doesn't make any difference whether you press once or twice – the significance is the same – but let it last for about two seconds. You are sharing the breath of life, and from now on you are more than just a visitor; you belong to the tangata whenua. If you wish, you can combine the hongi with a handshake and a greeting such as 'Tēnā koe' or 'Kia ora!'

Māori express: 30 words to know and understand

We use a lot of Māori words in New Zealand English in a natural and unselfconscious way. Greetings at the start of a news bulletin on TV, for example, are often in Māori. It's one of the features of New Zealand English that makes it distinctive and interesting. Here are a few examples.

aroha	love, affection, compassion, empathy
haka	posture dance usually performed by males; dance of challenge and welcome
hāngī	food cooked in an earth oven
hīkoi	a walk or march with others going in the same direction for the same purpose; a protest march
hui	meeting or conference
ka pai!	very good; well done!
kai	food
kapa haka	Māori cultural group
kaumātua	an elder of the tribe
koha	gift, donation, contribution
kōrero	discussion
kuia	a female elder
mana	prestige, authority, influence, spiritual power, charisma
Māoritanga	things that relate directly to Māori values and concepts
marae	traditional meeting place
moko	traditional tattoo on the face or body
mokopuna	grandchild or young person
Pākehā	people of European origin; non-Māori

pounamu	greenstone
tamariki	children
tāne	man, husband
tangata whenua	'people of the land'; original people belonging to a place, local people, hosts
taniwha	guardian; legendary monster; may interrupt road works unless suitably appeased
taonga	treasured possessions or cultural items
tikanga Māori	the Māori way of doing things, practices, conventions
tūrangawaewae	the place where you have the right to live because of kinship and whakapapa
wahine	woman, wife
waka	canoe, vehicle or airplane; sometimes used figuratively to mean a political party
whakapapa	genealogy, genealogical table
whānau	extended family group

SAY G'DAY: MĀORI GREETINGS

Mōrena	(Good) Morning!
Pō mārie	Good night!
Kia ora	Hello (informal)
Kia ora koutou	Hello everybody (informal)
Tēnā koe	Hello (to one person – formal)
Tēnā koutou	Hello (to more than two people – formal)
Tēnā tātou katoa	Greetings! (to everybody present – formal)
Haere mai	Welcome!
Haere rā	Goodbye (from the person staying)
E noho rā	Goodbye (from the person leaving)
Ka kite anō	See you later

Saving a national treasure

Two hundred years ago, you would have heard more Māori language (te reo Māori) spoken in this country than English. With the arrival of more and more settlers, however, the dominance of the Māori language diminished. Back then, the Māori language wasn't appreciated as an essential tool for preserving culture, and its use in schools was actively discouraged. By the middle of the 20th century, te reo Māori was badly in need of maintenance; unless strenuous efforts were put into protecting and revitalising it, the Māori language would die out.

In 1985, the Waitangi Tribunal declared that the Māori language was a taonga (treasure) that the government had a duty to protect under the Treaty of Waitangi. On 1 August 1987, by Act of Parliament, te reo Māori became an official language of New Zealand.

According to the 2013 Census, 21.3 percent of Māori could hold a conversation about a lot of everyday things in te reo Māori, down from 26.1 percent in the 2006 Census.

How do you say that?

Ngaruawahia, pīpīwharauroa, pōhutukawa, pounamu, Whakarewarewa . . . In New Zealand, many of our placenames, as well as the names of birds, animals and trees, are Māori in origin, so it's worth learning a little about pronunciation.

Luckily, te reo Māori has consistent rules. By remembering these, the words that look like tongue-twisters are easily pronounced.

- There are five vowels and ten consonants in the Māori alphabet.
  Vowels: *a, e, i, o, u*
  Consonants: *h, k, m, n, p, r, t* and *w,* plus two diagraphs (two letters that combine to form one sound): wh and ng.
  '*Wh*' is pronounced like the 'f' in 'father'.
  '*Ng*' is pronounced like the 'ng' in 'singer' (but not like the 'ng' in 'finger').

- The vowels can be long or short. A long vowel sound is marked by a macron (a line over the vowel); e.g. 'ā' in Māori.
- The eight consonants are pronounced the same way as they are in English.
- Each syllable is stressed equally (unlike in English, which puts stress on certain syllables).
- Māori words do not take an 's' to form the plural.

A very helpful pronunciation guide (in either a male or female voice) is available online at: hedc.otago.ac.nz/whakahuatanga

Modern Māori: te reo evolves

Just like other languages, te reo Māori has to create new words to keep up with modern concepts, activities and technologies.

The Māori Language Commission is the official source of new Māori equivalents of English words: if you want the word for 'pizza', for example, or maybe 'ping-pong' or 'defensive driving', the Commission will do an exhaustive search to check that the Māori equivalent doesn't already exist and, if not, it will coin a new word that retains the cultural integrity of te reo. The new word will be peer-reviewed before it and its derivation are entered into an electronic database of neologisms.

The Māori word for 'pizza', by the way, is 'parehe' – found in Herbert Williams' *Dictionary of the Māori Language*, it means 'flat cake of meal from fern root'.

The word for 'ping-pong' is poikōpiko – from 'poi', meaning 'ball', and 'kōpiko', which means 'go alternately in opposite directions'.

The Māori equivalent for 'defensive driving' is 'karo aituā waka', from 'karo', meaning 'avoid'; 'aituā', meaning 'misfortune, trouble, disaster, accident'; and 'waka', meaning 'vehicle'.

Social media platforms such as Twitter have spawned many new words. The word 'tīhau', which means 'the chirp of a bird', was selected as the equivalent of 'tweet', and the word 'paetīhau' was the obvious equivalent for 'Twitter': 'the perch or platform from where a bird tweets'.

Delivering the message: Whina Cooper's hīkoi

In days gone by, the New Zealand Government had a shameful habit of 'acquiring' land that didn't by rights belong to it. Despite the fact that, by 1939, Māori held only 1 percent of the South Island and 9 percent of the North Island, the Crown continued its land grab for several more decades. But it couldn't continue without dire consequences for Māori, who have a special relationship with the land.

At 9.30am on 14 September 1975, respected Māori leader Whina Cooper left Te Hapua in the Far North, hand in hand with her three-year-old granddaughter. A few months short of her 80th birthday, this passionately determined woman walked all the way to Wellington to express opposition to any further alienation of Māori land. Along the way she galvanised support, and by the time she reached Parliament 30 days later, the hīkoi (protest march) was 5000 strong.

Whina Cooper presented a petition to Prime Minister Bill Rowling, demanding that 'not one more acre' of Māori land be taken.

A few days later, on 10 October 1975, Parliament passed the Treaty of Waitangi Act, which created the Waitangi Tribunal, which continues to investigate Māori grievances connected with the Treaty to this day.

LOCAL KNOWLEDGE

The longest Māori placename in New Zealand

If you go to Hawke's Bay, drive south from Waipukurau for about 55 kilometres, then turn right and drive for another 5 kilometres. You'll find a rather ordinary-looking little hill that is world famous for its remarkably long name.

The signpost reads 'Taumata whakatangi hangakoauau o tamatea turi pukakapiki maunga horo nuku pokai whenua kitanatahu', which means 'the place where Tamatea, the man with the big knees, who slid, climbed and swallowed mountains, known as "landeater", played his flute to his loved one'. Most people simplify things by calling it Taumata Hill.

The signpost makes an interesting photo, but the hill itself is on privately owned land and you need to get permission first if you want to walk up it.

The 'Ka mate!' haka and its baby brother

Some of the most readily recognised words in Māori belong to the haka 'Ka mate', the challenge dance performed by the All Blacks before a rugby test match. It has been a prematch ritual for the team for well over a century; it was introduced to the rugby pitch by the 'Originals', who toured Britain in 1905–06 and won all but one of their matches.

The All Blacks' attention to correct form varied a bit over the years until Buck Shelford became captain in 1987. He insisted on getting the haka right, doing it with meaning, and being certain of the effect. As a result, the haka is a mesmerising spectacle. It unsettles the opposition, stirs up patriotic fervour in the spectators, and primes the players for the confrontation that will follow.

Ā, ka mate! Ka mate!	Tis death! Tis death!
Ka ora! Ka ora!	Tis life! Tis life!
Ka mate! Ka mate!	Tis death! Tis death!
Ka ora! Ka ora!	Tis life! Tis life!
Tēnei te tangata	Behold there stands
pūhuruhuru	the hairy man
Nāna nei i tiki mai	Who will cause
whakawhiti te rā	the sun to shine!
Ā, upane!	One step upwards!
Ā, ka upane!	Another step upwards!
Ā, hupane! Ka upane!	One step upwards! Another step upwards!
Whiti te rā, hī!	The sun shines!

Particularly when performed by the All Blacks, the gestures and posturing deliver a ferocious message – even though the precise meaning of the words is a bit of a mystery to most.

'Ka mate' was composed about 200 years ago by Te Rauparaha, a famous Ngāti Toa fighting chief. It celebrates his very good fortune when he avoided his enemies and escaped death by hiding in a pit used for storing kūmara (sweet potato).

With all the talk of life and death and lines like 'There stands / the hairy man / who will cause / the sun to shine', it was hardly surprising that some wondered what the All Blacks were on about. Yes, sport is certainly a passion in New Zealand, but even we will admit that it's not usually a matter of life and death. 'Ka mate' had been central to All Black tradition for a hundred years, but as we eased into a new millennium, the time seemed right to have a haka that related more to what the boys were actually doing out on the field.

Enter Ngāti Porou's Derek Lardelli, a renowned tā moko (traditional tattooing) artist and cultural advisor. In 2005, he composed a new haka, 'Kapa o Pango', to be the younger brother of 'Ka mate'. When the All Blacks debuted it on 27 August 2005 against South Africa at Carisbrook in Dunedin, unprepared spectators were shocked. When Piri Weepu, the halfback, drew his finger across his throat in what appeared to be an unmistakable depiction of throat-slitting, it seemed a bit unsportsmanlike.

Derek Lardelli was quick to explain. This haka was not a war dance, he said, but a ceremony. This haka was about building spiritual, physical and intellectual capacity before doing something very important. 'It says, "This is my time to express myself in the black jersey on behalf of my country."' The questionable gesture was simply about pulling energy from the left to the right side of the body, through the heart and lungs. (The All Blacks, by the way, won that match, 31–27.)

Kapa o Pango kia whakawhenua au i ahau!	Let me become one with the land
Hī aue, hī! Ko Aotearoa e ngunguru nei!	It is New Zealand that thunders now
Au, au, aue hā!	And it is my time! It is my moment!
Ko Kapa o Pango e ngunguru nei!	This defines us as the All Blacks
Au, au, aue hā!	And it is my time! It is my moment!
I āhaha! Ka tū te ihiihi	The anticipation explodes! Feel the power!
I āhahā!	It is my time! It is my moment!
Ka tū te ihiihi	Our dominance
Ka tū te wanawana	Our supremacy will triumph
Ki runga ki te rangi e tū iho nei, tū iho nei, hī!	And will be placed on high
Ponga rā!	Silver fern!
Kapa o Pango, aue hī!	All Blacks!
Ponga rā!	Silver fern!
Kapa o Pango, aue hī, hā!	All Blacks!

For more about the All Blacks and their haka, visit: www.allblacks.com

Chapter four

KIWIS:
THE
PEOPLE

The perks of being a Kiwi

Most New Zealanders – 87 percent of us – reported in the 2012 New Zealand General Social Survey that life, on the whole, was pretty sweet. Satisfaction levels were higher than the OECD average, and on a par with Australia, the US and Canada. Why?

1. We're free to roam.
Our isolation has its compensations, but sometimes we just need to see what the rest of the world is like. That's the beauty of the New Zealand passport: it opens the door to 168 countries, without the need for a visa.

2. We've got no real problems with the neighbours.
We may not look too friendly with each other on the sports field, but the Australians do allow us to live, work or study in their country for as long as we want.

3. We've got a decent amount of personal space.
The number of people per square kilometre in the UK is 258; in New Zealand, it's 16 – in other words, we have 15 times the elbow room.

4. When you want something done, you don't need to offer officials envelopes stuffed with cash.
Bribery is not a way of life in New Zealand; in fact, the value we place on transparency means we've been identified as one of the world's least corrupt countries.

5. Paradise is just a little north.
For the rest of the world, all those gorgeous tropical islands of Oceania are an eternity away. Flying from New Zealand, we hardly have time for a meal and a movie before touching down.

6. You can head off into nature without tripping over dangerous snakes, scorpions – or bears.

There are three spiders to watch out for – the katipō, the redback and the white tail – but it's nice to know that you can snuggle into your sleeping bag at the end of the day without finding anything nasty has slithered in before you.

7. We weren't founded on a class system, so societal divisions are about as blurry as human nature and the capitalist system will allow.

We believe in a fair go – the Waitangi Tribunal, the Disputes Tribunal (formerly the Small Claims Court) and the Ombudsman are examples of that. And we don't stand on ceremony: we address each other by our first names as soon as we meet.

8. Once we are dressed for the day, that's pretty much it.

We don't have to add or remove endless layers, as people do when they heat their houses to temperatures 50 degrees warmer than it is outside. The difference between the average daily high and the average daily low in most New Zealand locations is less than 10 degrees Celsius.

9. It's so much easier to be a big fish in a little pond.

A small population means fewer employment opportunities, but the competition is less, and it's easier to rise to the top once you've got the job. It's also easier to get your picture in the paper or your face on the telly.

10. We're at peace with ourselves and with the rest of the world.

Ask any new arrival from Afghanistan, Iraq or other conflict-weary country how good that feels. Police officers on routine patrols don't carry guns, nor do security officials in the country's airports. In the annual Global Peace Index study, New Zealand consistently ranks among the three most peaceful countries in the world, along with Iceland and Denmark.

11. The food tastes good, because much of it is grown locally and does not have too far to travel to get to the markets.

12. Voting in elections is optional, and there is more than one party to choose from.

If you choose not to participate, there are no fines to pay. At the general election in November 2011, only 74.21 percent of eligible voters cast a vote, one of the lowest turnouts in the country's history.

13. As long as you don't mind a wait, affordable medical help is a reality.

Doctor's visits are free for kids under six years of age; accident and emergency treatment at public hospitals is also free. Although there can be long waiting lists for elective surgery, hospital treatment is free in the public system, and treatment by specialists is subsidised.

14. You can also get an education without borrowing from the bank.

All three- and four-year-olds are eligible to receive 20 hours of free early childhood education each week. After that, schooling is free at state schools and state integrated schools, although parents are expected to pay a 'donation' of up to $1000.

15. Visits from relatives you have cheerfully left behind in the UK, Europe, North America or anywhere else more than a 3-hour flight away are usually few and far between.

If we're honest, it *is* quite a long way to come, and the cost of bringing a family of four makes even the fondest family members hesitate before writing to let you know they're on their way.

16. Whatever you want to do, it's likely to be close by.

As well as world-class shopping, theatre, restaurants, museums and visitor attractions, we've got mountains, lakes, rivers, beaches and bush. City parks are generally free of polluted waterways, potholed roads and menacing dogs.

17. There is no compulsory military service.
When you leave school or university, you can get stuck into a career without first spending years dressed up in uniform. Service in the New Zealand Armed Forces is voluntary.

18. It's easy to get a view of the sea.
The furthest you can get from the coastline is 120 kilometres. In some parts of the US, you could travel almost 20 times that before dipping your toes in the water.

19. We get to host royal tours.
Some people squawk that the monarchy is irrelevant to the Kiwi lifestyle, and that picking up the tab for a royal visit is a waste of money, but most of us love the fact that Queen Elizabeth II has done us proud for over 60 years, and we will turn up anytime there's an opportunity for a 'meet and greet'. Magazines featuring royalty on the cover still outsell any other issues.

20. Others love us.
Our peacefulness, friendliness, cleanliness and general lack of pretension are very endearing. The Australians may laugh at our accent, but the Americans think it's kind of cute.

Parallel universe: what's so funny?

On 12 April 1978, during BBC radio programme *Quote... Unquote*, the English humorist and radio personality Clement Freud was asked what his impressions of New Zealand were. 'I find it hard to say,' he responded, 'because when I was there it seemed to be shut.'

We felt a bit hurt and misunderstood. Back then, New Zealand was regarded as what Britain would have been like three decades previously – rather quiet and somewhat dull. But things have changed, and the differences between us and the rest of the world have been minimised. Or have they? Let's eavesdrop on some of the thoughts of recent arrivals . . .

Sarawut, from Thailand: Things seemed very different as soon as I got off the plane. Inside the airport, there was a small dog that sniffed its way through all the suitcases that were coming out on the luggage carousel.

Roshan, from Sri Lanka: About a month after I arrived in Wellington, I was invited by some new Kiwi friends to their place for a meal. I was asked to bring a plate. I thought it was a bit strange, but my friends had just moved into a new home, and I assumed they must be short of crockery. Some other guests arrived at the front door at the same time as I did. When they'd stopped laughing and explained that 'bring a plate' meant I should have brought some food, they gave me some of the sandwiches they'd brought to put on my plate, so that I didn't look like a major idiot. In Sri Lanka, we have servants to do the meal preparation, so taking food to a party would be an insult to someone's hospitality.

Méi Lán, from China: In Guangzhou, I lived on the 23rd floor of an apartment block. When I came to New Zealand, I felt I was in a fairyland: all those separate red, green and blue roofs were beautiful! In China, if I could see any roofs at all, they were all concrete and were covered in washing lines and air-conditioning units.

José, from Mexico: In my country, the side of the road is covered in rubbish. Here, it's so tidy! You don't even see a decent dead dog.

Barney, from England: I managed to get two parking tickets within my first month of being here. It took me that long to learn that parking on the right-hand side of the road is illegal. In London, you can pull in on either side of the road, just wherever there's a space.

Zaki, from Iraq: When I was new here, some Kiwi classmates invited me to 'come for tea'. I thought seven o'clock seemed a bit late to sit and drink tea, but I was so happy to be making some new friends that I happily went along. I got a huge surprise when they served up a full evening meal.

Robert, from Jamaica: I couldn't believe how much Kiwis talk about the weather, but I suppose that's because it changes all the time and you can't help noticing it. In Jamaica, the weather is really stable, so there's not that much to say about it.

Isabella, from Argentina: I stopped at a roadside fruit stall just out of Auckland and bought some apples. I then saw a sign that said 'Free Range Eggs', so I helped myself and went back to my car. I was startled to see somebody chasing after me, waving their arms. What I got for free was an English lesson, but not the eggs.

Aslan, from Turkey: Kiwi guys thought I was gay, because they saw me kiss my

Turkish mates on both cheeks when we said hello. In New Zealand, apart from a handshake, there isn't a lot of male-to-male physical contact – unless it's to hug the guy in your rugby team who's just scored a try.

Marieke, from Holland: I was impressed to see that Māori culture seemed to be respected. However, I was surprised to notice most people couldn't speak Māori, despite free classes being available. In any European country with more than one official language, kids are taught both languages at school very early and can often speak both fluently by the time they graduate.

Anna-Lise, from France: I found it very odd the way people interact with each other without being friends or relatives. The first few times a shop assistant called me 'love' or 'darling', I got offended. In France, you would never, ever use such terms for someone you don't know personally. But after I got used to it, I thought it was actually quite nice.

Suzie, from the US: You don't have to tip somebody every time you turn around. Oh, the joy!

Wilson, from South Africa: At the first staff meeting I went to in my new job at the bank, I looked around and noticed how many different nationalities were represented. In South Africa, racial differences make us nervous – it always feels as though there's potential for trouble – but here, it was as though nobody even noticed it. It's a joyful thing.

Dani, from Israel: I grew up on a kibbutz with about 300 other people. The meals were very predictable, and most of the food we grew ourselves. Here, you can find all sorts of ethnic restaurants. I've tried Thai food for the first time, as well as Indian and Japanese. There are so many new flavours to sample. I'm still not sure what 'Kiwi food' actually is.

How 'Kiwi' became our cultural ID

Before the 20th century, the kiwi was just one of various symbols used on banknotes, postage stamps and army badges, or in cartoons, to represent New Zealand. It took the loving tribute of an Australian to popularise the term to describe New Zealanders. In 1906, William Ramsay invented a shoe polish and decided to name it after the kiwi in honour of his wife's birthplace. Kiwi Shoe Polish was sold in the UK and the US during World War I, and was widely used by soldiers to keep their boots clean and shiny.

It was only a small shift for the Allied soldiers to apply the name of their boot polish to their comrades from New Zealand. Perhaps the New Zealand soldiers were proud to be associated with such an idiosyncratic creature. In any case, the soldiers who occupied Sling Camp on Salisbury Plain in England during World War I carved a giant kiwi on the chalk hill above their wooden huts. Before long, New Zealand soldiers were widely known as 'Kiwis'.

In World War II, New Zealand soldiers again got the 'Kiwi' nickname – and it not only stuck, it spread. It came to be used to describe any New Zealander, not just soldiers. We didn't mind. Because the kiwi is the only bird of its kind, we decided it suited us rather well and we have held on to the name fondly ever since.

Meet some Kiwis: 20 names you may need to know

Why isn't Ed Hillary on this list, you may ask? Or Ernest Rutherford, or Katherine Mansfield or hundreds – if not thousands – of other world-famous Kiwis? The answer is this: New Zealand's Hall of Fame is very fully occupied, and you will find a great number of books that tell the story of those men and women who shaped our history and who we are so proud of.

The names below are some of those that might pop up in the news or during a casual conversation. These people are not our national heroes, and their fame may be fleeting, but equipped with a bit of background, you'll be able to join in the chat. They are listed in no particular order, apart from alphabetical.

WOMEN

Alison Mau   Popular and accomplished TV and radio journalist, who took the country by surprise twice: first when she separated from her husband (a fellow news reader) and second, when, a couple of years later, she came out as bisexual and became engaged to dance teacher Karleen Edmonds.

Celia Lashlie   The first female prison officer to work in a male prison, and formerly the manager of Christchurch Women's Prison. Now a best-selling writer known for changing our thinking on the best ways to bring up our boys.

Georgina Beyer Worked as a drag queen and sex worker before entering politics as Mayor of Carterton. She was voted into Parliament in 1999, and became the world's first transsexual MP.

Helen Clark New Zealand's first elected female prime minister, who served three consecutive terms (1999–2008). Now Administrator of the United Nations Development Programme, the first woman to lead the organisation.

Karen Walker Very cool, internationally successful fashion designer worn by the likes of Kelly Osbourne, Sienna Miller, Liv Tyler, Claire Danes and Tyra Banks. Her signature look is tailored, almost androgynous.

Kerre McIvor (née Woodham) Talkback radio host, writer of books and media columns, public speaker. She called one of her autobiographies *Short Fat Chick to Marathon Runner*. Climbed Mount Kilimanjaro for charity in 2013.

Parris Goebel Self-taught hip hop dancer and choreographer, named Young New Zealander of the Year in 2014. Still in her early 20s, she and her dance crew have won the Hip Hop Megacrew title for three years in a row. She has choreographed for Cirque du Soleil, as well as for a Jenifer Lopez tour.

Rachel Hunter Found fame as a teenager by starring in an ice cream advertisement on TV. Went on to marry (and divorce) superstar Rod Stewart. Lives in Los Angeles but remains a Kiwi at heart and frequently comes home. A popular judge on *New Zealand's Got Talent*.

Dame Rosie Horton	A dedicated philanthropist whose charitable work over the last 40 years has helped raise millions of dollars for Starship Children's Hospital, as well as the arts, the disabled, the environment, and women and children's charities.
Valerie Adams	Four-time world champion shot-putter who was denied a gold medal at the London Olympics in 2012 until Belarus shot-putter Nadzeya Ostapchuk was discovered to be a drugs cheat. Valerie became the only person to be handed an Olympic medal on New Zealand soil.

MEN

Colin Mathura-Jeffree	A model of Anglo-Indian ethnicity, judge for *New Zealand's Next Top Model* and host of *New Zealand's Hottest Home Baker*, who adds a highly decorative element to his TV programmes as well as to the multitude of society events he attends.
Sir John Kirwan	Legendary All Blacks winger and former coach of Japan and Italy national rugby teams, now known for his work raising awareness of depression and other mental health issues. Voted the person Kiwis trust the most in a 2013 poll conducted by *Reader's Digest*.
Len Brown	Mayor of the Auckland 'supercity', whose support for holding this powerful position nosedived when details of a tawdry two-year affair with Bevan Chuang, a Chinese woman more than 20 years his junior, came to light just after he was re-elected. Refused to resign, despite public scorn and derision.

Nigel Latta	Psychologist and presenter of two popular TV series, including *The Politically Incorrect Parenting Show*, which reassured parents about managing their difficult teenagers.
Richard Faull	World-class scientist whose discoveries have made it possible to start looking for ways to enhance the brain's own efforts to repair the damage inflicted by strokes or disease. Loves the challenge of using the brain to understand the brain.
Sir Richard Taylor	Holder of five Academy Awards for work produced through his Weta Workshop, a special effects and props company central to the success of *The Lord of the Rings*, *King Kong*, *Avatar* and *The Hobbit*.
Richie McCaw	Legendary rugby player who made his international debut against Ireland in 2001 and went on to captain the All Blacks to victory at the 2011 Rugby World Cup. For his efforts, he was offered a knighthood, but modestly turned it down.
Sam Hunt	Nationally loved poet who, through pub-based performances and a slightly shambolic clothes sense, made it acceptable for Kiwi blokes to enjoy the rhythm of words. Famous for his love of the bottle, his word-perfect recall of thousands of poems and his line: 'Tell the story, tell it true, charm it crazy.'
Sam Johnson	Used Facebook to galvanise a student volunteer army after the Canterbury earthquakes in February 2011. His helpers gave 75,000 hours of their time to scrape up liquefaction sludge and provide food and water to distressed residents. Young New Zealander of the Year in 2012.

Winston Peters   Leader of the New Zealand First party known for his dazzling smile, his infuriating tactics and his support among elderly voters. To the dismay of other political parties, he regularly finds himself holding the balance of power after a national election.

Who's that in your wallet? The faces on our banknotes

$5	Sir Edmund Hillary (1919–2008). In 1953 he became the first man to climb Mount Everest, and in 1958 he was the first man to drive overland to the South Pole
$10	Kate Sheppard (1848–1934). Spearheaded the campaign to give women the vote in New Zealand; in 1893 New Zealand became the first country in the world to give all people the vote
$20	Queen Elizabeth II (1926–). The portrait on the banknote was taken in Wellington in 1986; the Queen is wearing the Sovereign's Badge of the Order of New Zealand
$50	Sir Apirana Ngata (1874–1950). The first Māori to graduate from a New Zealand university; an MP for 38 years and an inspirational leader
$100	Ernest, Lord Rutherford of Nelson (1871–1937). Internationally recognised as the 'father of nuclear physics' and winner of the Nobel Prize in Chemistry in 1908

LOCAL KNOWLEDGE

What is Red Socks Day all about?

Peter Blake was an outstanding Kiwi yachtsman and environmental advocate. One of his achievements was successfully contesting the America's Cup twice, winning it in 1995 and defending it in 2000.

During the 1995 America's Cup campaign, Blake wore a pair of red socks given to him by his wife, Pippa. The only time Blake wasn't on board wearing his red socks, the Kiwis lost the race. The socks became a nationally recognised good luck charm and, from then on, Kiwis in their thousands put on their own red socks to show their support.

Peter Blake was murdered by pirates in the Amazon in 2001 while he was on an environmental mission. In July each year, Red Socks Day is when we remember him and celebrate the true meaning of leadership. For details, see: www.sirpeterblaketrust.org/get-involved/red-socks-day

On 30 June 2011, Governor-General Anand Satyanand and a team of volunteers pegged 25,128 red socks on more than 3 kilometres of clothes-line strung up in Wellington's 'Cake Tin' sports stadium. Their effort secured a Guinness World Record, and the Sir Peter Blake Trust is now the official record holder for the longest clothes-line of socks.

Chapter five

HOW TO BE MISTAKEN FOR A KIWI

How to sound like a Kiwi

Kiwis speak fast, run words together, and mumble. We say *eh* and *y'know* all the time, and our vowel sounds transmute into something almost comical: Australians tell us that when we want to buy six fish, we ask for 'sucks fush'; we often grow our own 'veeegtabulls'; and when we agree with something we say 'yiss'. If you ask us to say *pan*, *pen* and *pin*, we will come out with something almost unrecognisable.

What's even more baffling is that we habitually let our sentences go up at the end, even when we're not asking a question. This feature is called the 'high-rising terminal'. If you ask us where the nearest bank is, we might say 'You go down here for a block (↑), and then you cross over (↑), and you'll see it along a bit on the right (↑).' You might feel puzzled because although we appear to be delivering detailed information, we sound so uncertain. What we're really doing is trying to connect with you and check up on your feelings. We are asking for reassurance that we are delivering the information you want, and that we share the same understanding of what is being said.

If you'd like to be cheerfully bamboozled by the peculiarities of the Kiwi accent, search in the local library for a book published in 1966 called *New Zild and How to Speak It* by Arch Acker. It opens with the friendly greeting 'Air gun?' ('How are you going?') and explains what we really mean when we start a question with 'Air Mice Poster' ('Air mice poster sleep while you keep making all that noise?'). Be warned: if you ask us 'Do you speak English?', we're likely to answer 'Ear sick horse!'

How to talk like a Kiwi

The English language has taken some novel twists and turns in New Zealand, and there are quite few expressions that you'll hear in ordinary conversation that have a not always obvious meaning. Here's a starter pack of local lingo . . .

anklebiter   a toddler

Aussie   an Australian, or the country itself

barbie   barbecue – the most popular summertime format for entertaining friends and family

booze bus   a roadside checkpoint where police stop drivers to check if they have been drinking alcohol

box of fluffy ducks   healthy and happy; if someone asks how you are, you can always reply 'A box of fluffy ducks, mate!'

bush   an area of native forest

chateau cardboard   wine sold in a cardboard wine box – regarded as a last port in a storm for cash-strapped picnickers

cheerios   little cocktail sausages in bright red casings; a popular staple at children's birthday parties, where they are served with a bowl of tomato sauce for dipping

couch kūmara   a person who sits on the couch watching television for hour after hour, no more animated than the vegetable itself. ('Kūmara' is the Māori word for sweet potato.)

ding   a slight indentation on your car as a result of impact with another car or a fixed object such as a garden wall

doer upper	a house that requires 'doing up' – i.e. needs repairs or renovation – often used in real estate advertisements
eggs benny	eggs Benedict, an item on brunch menus nationwide. Eggs florry (Florentine) is similar, but served with wilted spinach
electric pūhā	marijuana. Conventional 'pūhā' is a green vegetable found in New Zealand, often served with roast pork. The electric version is used entirely differently, apparently for recreational purposes
extra curly	particularly well; a suitable response if somebody asks you how you are and you want to indicate that you're feeling happy and energetic. Contrasts with plain '**curly**', which refers to a question that is difficult to answer or a situation that is difficult to resolve.
fair go	a situation where both sides' reasonable expectations are met; for example: 'I don't think it's a fair go expecting me to clear up all your mess.' A long-standing popular TV programme called *Fair Go* tackles consumer complaints, seeking justice for anyone who's been given a **raw deal** (which is the opposite of a fair go)
fair suck of the kūmara	if you're not getting a fair suck of the kūmara, you're not being treated fairly
flash	flash clothes or a flash restaurant might be regarded with suspicion as being excessively sophisticated or fashionable. On the other hand, if you 'don't feel too flash', you don't feel very well
go flatting	to leave your parents' home to live independently either in a flat (shared accommodation) or a house
go hard out	to do something at full intensity
good on ya, mate!	probably of Aussie origin, it means you've done well and I like your attitude
hard case	someone whose behaviour verges on excessive but who is nevertheless entertaining is a 'hard case'

JAFA — acronym for the derogatory expression 'Just another f— Aucklander'. Not to be confused with 'jaffa', a popular orange-coated chocolate sweet

like a possum in the headlights — immobilised with fear, like the animal that sees the headlights of an oncoming car and can't move off the road, due to fear

long drop — a rudimentary outdoor toilet consisting of a small cabin with a wooden seat built over a hole in the ground

Mainlanders — what South Islanders like to call themselves

mate's rates — a discounted price for goods or services offered to friends

Maussie — a Māori who lives in Aussie (Australia). Pronounced the same way as, but not to be confused with, the term '**mozzie**', the abbreviation for 'mosquito'

mental health day — a day off work, taken not because you're physically sick but because you feel that time spent relaxing would be beneficial to your attitude; don't expect your employer to sympathise or approve

munted — broken or ruined. Used, for example, to describe a smartphone no longer functioning after it has been accidentally dropped into the toilet bowl

Nippon clip-ons — in 1966, Japanese engineers devised a way to add extension lanes on either side of the Auckland harbour bridge. What else could they be called?

no worries — if you ask someone a favour and they respond with 'No worries', they are agreeing to help you

normal school — the existence of normal schools does not imply that other schools are abnormal or subnormal. A 'normal school' is one that is attached to a teacher training college so trainee teachers can be supervised as they gain experience

OE	the abbreviation for 'overseas experience' – an extended working holiday abroad, usually for a year or two after graduating from university, and often starting in London, England. Also referred to as **'the big OE'**
on the dole	receiving the government unemployment benefit, now euphemistically termed 'Jobseeker Support'
open home	the time when a real estate agent supervises the general public's inspection of a house for sale
Red Shed	an affectionate nickname for The Warehouse, a chain of retail stores that specialises in low-cost items
Remuera tractor	a snide nickname for a sports utility vehicle, regarded as an unnecessarily ostentatious car in which to pick up children from school, visit the supermarket, or drive through expensive Auckland suburbs
sausage sizzle	a fundraising barbecue where sausages are cooked on the **'barbie'**, wrapped in white bread and sold (with the option of fried onions and tomato sauce) for a dollar or two
she'll be right	everything will be okay; sometimes abbreviated to 'she's right'
she's a hard road	it's a bit of a challenge
shonky	poor quality, unreliable, dishonest – might refer to a piece of equipment; might equally refer to an accountant or lawyer
shout	if it's your shout at the pub, then it's your turn to buy a round of drinks for everybody.
stunned mullet	a person who is paralysed by shock; their expression is similar to that of a fish that has been clubbed after being caught – or a **'possum in the headlights'**

sweet as	similar to 'awesome' or 'choice', to describe something as 'cool', and completely okay
take an early shower	to be sent off the sports field for being unsportspersonlike. You'll know it's your turn to head for the changing room when the ref holds up a red card
the big one	a term to describe a severe earthquake that citizens of Wellington fear will inevitably occur one day
the Men in Black	the All Blacks, the much beloved national rugby team, winners of the 2011 Rugby World Cup (just in case you'd forgotten)
tiki tour	the unnecessarily long way from Point A to Point B: taxi drivers are sometimes suspected of taking tourists on a tiki tour between the airport and their hotel, in order to earn a better fare
waka jumper	a politician who switches their support from one party to another
yeah, right	a sarcastic snort of disbelief. The phrase became popular following a series of topical billboard advertisements for Tui beer; for example: 'Let's take a moment this Christmas to think about Christ.' 'Yeah, right'

LOCAL KNOWLEDGE

Stamping ground

In July 2007, New Zealand Post issued a set of 20 stamps called 'Classic Kiwi'. Each stamp highlighted a typically Kiwi expression, such as 'good as gold' or 'away with the fairies'. By holding your finger on the black portion of any of the stamps, through the magic of heat-sensitive ink, the 'English translation' was revealed.

LOCAL KNOWLEDGE: A HANDY TRANSLATOR

ITEM	NEW ZEALAND WORD	AUSTRALIAN EQUIVALENT
insulated box for keeping food cold	chilly bin	Esky (originally a trademark; now a generic term)
convenience store	dairy	milkbar or deli
bed quilt	duvet	doona
flip-flops	jandals	thongs
sweater	jersey	jumper
swimwear	togs	bathers
trousers	pants	daks, strides
holiday home	bach (in the North Island), crib (in the South Island)	beach house
walking through the countryside on foot	tramping	hiking
a raised section of road used to deter speeding	judder bar	speed bump

How to swear like a Kiwi

When Emirates Team New Zealand lost the 2013 America's Cup yacht race in San Francisco Bay after coming so tantalisingly close to winning, Prime Minister John Key tweeted a single word: 'Bugger'.

We're allowed to say this rude word, because the Advertising Standards Authority (ASA) says so. Back in 1999, the ASA had to consider a complaint about an advertisement on TV in which a series of farming mishaps caused by underestimating the power of a Toyota Hi-Lux Ute prompted the farmer–owner to express his disbelief using the same single potent word: 'Bugger!' Even the farm dog said it when he was left sprawling in the mud after missing his leap onto the back of the truck. (Watch the ad on YouTube: www.youtube.com/watch?v=TKY_OysWu3k.)

The ad raised eyebrows in more than a few suburban living rooms, but the ASA dismissed complaints by saying 'the usage of a Kiwi colloquialism is appropriate to the circumstances portrayed'. Losing the America's Cup by one miserable point created similarly appropriate circumstances.

By the way, if something is 'buggered', it's broken, exhausted or not able to function. The word may refer to a piece of machinery or to a person.

How to eat like a Kiwi

Over the last couple of decades, Kiwi taste has become astronomically more sophisticated, especially now we've learned to incorporate the flavour and flair of Pacific Rim cuisines. With the ready availability of ingredients that would have seemed impossibly exotic to our mothers, we're now more likely to whip up an aromatic, sizzling stir-fry than the traditional bland meat-and-three-veg formula that worked so well for so long. But despite the revolution, there are some foods that will be part of our repertoire forever.

Marmite sandwich: Marmite – a salty black yeast spread that contains folate and B vitamins – is probably the food that newcomers find most difficult to acclimatise to. Spread Marmite sparingly on buttered bread, or check out the Marmite Facebook page, where debate rages on the best way to enjoy it: www.facebook.com/MarmiteNZ

Roast lamb: For a good basic recipe for this classic Kiwi roast, check out the following website, which gives cooking times and methods: www.recipes.co.nz/roast-leg-of-lamb-with-rosemary

Whitebait fritter: Whitebait are the tiny, translucent young of various freshwater fish. They have little black eyes that you must ignore if you are to truly enjoy your fritter. During the whitebait season, they are cooked in a fritter or omelette. For a recipe, go to:
www.annabel-langbein.com/recipes/carols-whitebait-fritters/307/

Meat pie: We take pies so seriously that there is an annual National Pie Day, and a Supreme Pie Award that bakers up and down the country hotly contest each year. To find out where you can buy the prizewinning pies, visit:
www.nzbakels.co.nz/pie_awards_2013.cfm

Cheese rolls: A reconstructed cheese sandwich, probably not a favourite with heart-health specialists, but very popular for its comfort factor, particularly in the south of the South Island. You generously spread a cheese filling over a slice of bread, then roll the bread up and toast it under the grill. Before the toast burns and just as the cheese becomes deliciously melted, it's done. Try one at Dunedin Airport, or see the recipe at:
www.nzwomansweekly.co.nz/food/recipes/cheese-rolls

Anzac biscuits: Biscuits made with rolled oats, flour, desiccated coconut, sugar, butter and golden syrup (no eggs). There is a law that prevents the name 'Anzac' being used without permission, but Anzac biscuits are exempt, as long as they are made true to the original recipe and are referred to as Anzac 'biscuits' and never as 'cookies'. Read the real Anzac biscuit story at:
www.armymuseum.co.nz/kiwis-at-war/did-you-know/the-anzac-biscuit

Pavlova: A celebratory meringue-based dessert, which must have a crispy crust and a marshmallow (slightly chewy) interior. Traditionally topped with cream and sliced kiwifruit or summer berries. Celebrity chef Peter Gordon provides tips for the perfect pavlova at: www.is.gd/petergordon_pavlova

How to cook like a Kiwi

Traditional Māori cooking style involves laying down a hāngi (earth oven). Plenty of preparation time is required – as much as 5 hours. Look for detailed instructions at: www.maori.cl/Hangi.htm

1. Dig a large hole.

2. Make a fire using macrocarpa or similar long-burning wood. Heat some rocks on the fire until they are white hot: volcanic rocks are good for this, as they will heat without cracking and shattering.

3. Place the food – meats such as chicken and pork, and vegetables such as potatoes, pumpkin and kūmara – into wire baskets, keeping meat and vegetables separate.

4. Construct the hāngi in layers: first the hot rocks at the bottom of the pit, then the meat basket on top of the rocks, then the vegetable basket. Cover everything with wet cotton sheets, followed by a layer of wet hessian sacks. Use a shovel to cover everything over with soil, then leave the food to cook for several hours before uncovering and eating it.

Contemporary Kiwi cooking style doesn't involve the same amount of waiting. Basically, you put pretty much everything on the barbecue, prepare a couple of salads, have a drink while you turn the sausages and make sure you've invited a few friends around to enjoy the evening with you.

How to dress like a Kiwi

When former prime minister Helen Clark wore a trouser suit to a state dinner held during the visit of Queen Elizabeth II in 2002, the British press reared up in protest. How could anyone, they sniffed, think that trousers were good enough when Her Majesty had stepped out in a full-length gown with a tiara perched on her head? Helen Clark laughed the way any practical, down-to-earth Kiwi would. 'In New Zealand evening trousers are considered very elegant,' she said, 'and I'm fortunate enough to be able to wear them.'

For much of our history, we haven't dressed up in a spectacularly flash fashion. In recent years, Kiwi fashion designers such as Karen Walker and Trelise Cooper have turned heads on the international stage, but for most Kiwi women, chic designer clothing is to be looked at, desired, but probably not worn. Like the brown-feathered kiwi, we veer towards the monochromatic (frequently black), the possibly less-than-exciting, and anything in keeping with the relaxed attitude of practical people. On the high street, some Kiwis strive for a bit of colour and pizazz, but otherwise Kiwi clothing is comfortable, predictable and usually mass produced.

There are, however, a few items of clothing that are quintessentially Kiwi – most of which had their origins down on the farm. Take the Swanndri, for instance: usually referred to as a 'swannie', it is a woollen overshirt that reaches to mid thigh, with a lace-up or zip-up front and, sometimes, a drawstring hood. It's a wardrobe essential for any self-respecting farmer, hunter, fisherman or whitebaiter, because it's warm, waterproof and not too flash. It can be worn in town but looks much more at home in the bush or back country. The same goes for black singlets and gumboots. Jandals, however – the other Kiwi wardrobe essential – are worn absolutely everywhere.

LOCAL KNOWLEDGE

The black list

Many of New Zealand's national sports teams have the word 'black' as part of their names.

All Blacks	men's rugby union
Black Ferns	women's rugby union
Blackcaps	men's cricket
Black Sox	men's softball
Black Sticks	men's and women's field hockey
Ice Blacks	men's ice hockey
Tall Blacks	men's basketball
Wheel Blacks	wheelchair rugby
Black Fins	surf lifesaving
Iron Blacks	American football, or gridiron

Curious point no. 1
The national soccer team is called the All Whites.

Curious point no. 2
For a few months, the men's badminton team called itself the 'Black Cocks', until the International Badminton Federation put its foot down and the name was officially dropped.

How to be mistaken for a Kiwi

1. Be self-deprecating.

No matter what your achievements are, what riches you amass or how famous you become, stay humble and modest. Remember that our national hero, Sir Ed Hillary, when asked how it felt to conquer the world's tallest mountain, said simply: 'I had a moment of quiet satisfaction.'

2. Love sport – and admire those who put in the time and physical effort without complaining.

Respect team effort and loyalty as demonstrated by the All Blacks, the Silver Ferns or our America's Cup crew. Support any team that beats the Aussies.

3. Keep an eye out for your mates.

Loyalty is everything. Even our 'reluctant hero', Willie Apiata, who was awarded a Victoria Cross for heaving his injured comrade over his shoulders and running 70 metres with him across rocky terrain in the face of heavy enemy gunfire in Afghanistan, described his impulse as 'just what a man does for his mates'.

4. Feel connected to the land.

Māori have been doing this for centuries. It's not quite as developed in more recently arrived New Zealanders, but, at a bare minimum, we do place big importance on houses that have great 'indoor–outdoor flow'. Those with a properly evolved appreciation of nature head for the beach, the bush or other place of natural beauty as frequently as possible. Also, keep repeating how important it is to keep New Zealand 'clean and green'.

5. Be slightly ambivalent about New Zealand's independence.

Accept that it's reassuring to have political allies such as Australia and the US, but know that we can stand on our own two feet and compete perfectly respectably with bigger countries. Similarly, show respect for the English monarchy, but know in your heart that we'd be completely okay as a republic.

6. Don't be a girl.

Harden up. Understand that blokey attitudes are perfectly acceptable – in women as well as in men. On the other hand, if you do choke up or melt down, look at people like John Kirwan, a former All Black who revealed his struggles with depression and earned our trust and respect by the bucketload. See how he does it at: www.depression.org.nz

7. Stay relaxed.

Think 'she'll be right', keep your hair on, and avoid conflict with others by saying 'Let's agree to disagree'. It means we don't have to buy guns for ourselves.

8. DIY: Do It Yourself.

Make sure you acquire a few practical skills, put them to regular use, and admire them in others. One of our favourite TV advertisements is an anthropological study well worth viewing. It shows two young boys in their sandpit discussing their DIY plans for the weekend, and their scathing put-down of an Australian playmate who refuses to help. Watch it on YouTube at:
www.youtube.com/watch?v=nqRVqXMyzhM

9. Keep your jokes understated and relaxed.

Think: the black-singlet and gumboot-wearing Fred Dagg; the Māori singer, actor and comedian Billy T James; and author Barry Crump, whose laconic wit compensated for a troubled soul. Google them!

10. When you travel overseas, put a sticker of the New Zealand flag on your suitcase or backpack.

Take a survival pack with you containing Marmite, a couple of sachets of Wattie's tomato sauce, some Pineapple Lumps, a few Whittaker's Peanut Slabs, a box of Weet-Bix, some Vogel's bread and a packet of Bell teabags. Even though you can probably buy many of these items elsewhere in the world, travelling with them in your luggage shows you are an authentically homesick Kiwi.

Chapter six

KIWI: OUR NATIONAL BIRD

Quick kiwi facts

The kiwi is a nocturnal flightless bird that eats delectable forest treats such as worms, snails, caterpillars and centipedes, as well as berries, roots and fruit. It has solid bones (unlike most other birds, which have hollow bones) and has the largest egg-to-body weight ratio of any bird. The female is bigger than the male: it can weigh up to 3.3 kilograms (just over 7 pounds) and reaches about 45 centimetres (18 inches) in height. Most kiwis have just one mate, and mate for life.

A kiwi legend

At first glance, a kiwi doesn't look very promising. It has drab-coloured plumage, it can't fly, it sniffs around in the dark for worms, and it is known to have a rather nasty nature. You might wonder why we find such a quirky bird so impossibly endearing, especially when most of us have never even seen one in the wild.

Well, it's all to do with the forest god Tāne. According to Māori legend, the kiwi once lived high in the trees and had beautifully coloured wings. One day, Tāne asked several different birds if one of them would live on the forest floor to help save the trees from the ground bugs that were destroying them. One by one, the birds – the tūī, the pūkeko and the pīpīwharauroa (shining cuckoo) – made their feeble excuses. Only the kiwi agreed to Tāne's request, even though it meant losing his beautiful wings and colourful feathers and living on the damp forest floor. What's more, Tāne said to the kiwi, 'You will not be able to return to the forest roof and will never see the light of day again.' Kiwi looked at the sun for the last time and sadly whispered goodbye. As a reward for his sacrifice, Tāne decreed that the kiwi would become the best known and most loved bird of all.

Why not fly?

The scientific explanation for why kiwi can't fly is because they didn't need to. Kiwi have been in New Zealand for about 39 million years, and they had no real predators so no need for flight until people arrived about 800 years ago, bringing their pets and other pests with them. Kiwi nested in underground burrows, and their wings evolved into tiny, useless structures.

A dozen kiwi questions

1. How many kiwi are there in New Zealand?
About 70,000 in total.

2. How many kinds of kiwi are there?
There are five species, all endangered or vulnerable to extinction:
- the brown kiwi – the most common kiwi, found only in the North Island
- the rowi – the rarest kiwi, with a population of about 375 birds, found near Okarito on the West Coast
- the tokoeka – found only in the south of the South Island
- the great spotted kiwi – the species with the most stable population
- the little spotted kiwi – the smallest kiwi, weighing only about 1 kilogram.

3. Why are kiwi under threat of extinction?
Kiwi have no natural defences against predators such as dogs, cats, rats and stoats, and because they are flightless, escape is difficult. Ninety-five percent of kiwi in the wild are killed before they are old enough to breed.

4. What is being done to save kiwi?

Kiwis (people) are passionate about making sure that kiwi (birds) survive. Efforts to boost the population centre on three main activities: erecting predator-proof fences around kiwi nesting spots and setting traps for predators; hatching kiwi eggs in incubators and raising the chicks in safety; and carrying out scientific research into kiwi behaviour and genetics.

Currently, there are around 80 volunteer-based community groups assisting the recovery programme, as well as 12 facilities that incubate kiwi eggs and five Department of Conservation kiwi sanctuaries.

BNZ Operation Nest Egg has been going since 1994. It involves taking kiwi eggs from the wild and incubating them in safety until they hatch and the chicks are big enough to stand a better chance of surviving in the wild. Over 200 chicks are raised this way each year, most of them at Rotorua's Rainbow Springs Kiwi Encounter (more than 120 eggs a year) and Auckland Zoo (up to 25 eggs a year). Over 1000 kiwi chicks have been released through Operation Nest Egg. To find out more about the programme, visit:
www.kiwisforkiwi.org/what-we-do/how-were-saving-kiwi/

For more information about kiwi recovery efforts and to view or purchase a DVD on how to save kiwi, visit: www.kiwisforkiwi.org

5. Does removing their eggs upset kiwi?

Research done by Operation Nest Egg shows that removing eggs is not detrimental to kiwi. North Island brown kiwi do not rear their young because their chicks are instinctive feeders, so removing the eggs does not upset the parents.

6. What's the advantage in having such a long bill?

Kiwi have a fantastic sense of smell, second only to that of the condor. As it walks around, a kiwi will tap the ground with its bill, sniffing loudly as it pokes in the soil and forest litter, looking for worms or spiders. The sniffing is so loud that you can usually hear a kiwi before you see it. In the tip of the kiwi bill is a sensory organ that can detect vibrations from worms even 3–4 centimetres under the surface. Sometimes, to probe the soil more deeply, a kiwi will briefly leap into the air and use its body weight to bury its bill as far as possible.

7. How long can kiwi live?

Scientists are not absolutely certain, but they think a lifespan of 60 years is possible.

8. What do kiwi sound like?

The call of the kiwi is quite a shrill whistle that varies slightly between species. You can hear it online: go to www.radionz.co.nz/collections/birds and click on any of the three kiwi pictured. Radio New Zealand features a different bird call each week just before the 7am news. On one occasion, when introducing the little spotted kiwi, one mischievous broadcaster suggested the bird was known to his mates as 'Measles'.

9. What are kiwi feathers like?

The dense coat that keeps kiwi warm and dry consists of shaggy feathers that feel like the mane or tail of a horse. Māori made a prestigious kind of cloak that was woven with kiwi feathers.

10. What do kiwi smell like?

Have you noticed that nobody has tried to bottle 'parfum de kiwi'? Kiwi smell funny – a bit like mushrooms or, even worse, ammonia. The conspicuous smell unfortunately makes it easier for predators such as cats and dogs to locate them.

11. Can you keep a kiwi as a pet?

No, because kiwi are protected. Anyway, they are not the sort of creature that would ever snuggle onto your lap in front of the telly; in fact, they are distinctly unsociable, and the adult birds have a reputation for being aggressive. You can, though, 'adopt' a kiwi for around $100 a year. Many of the websites listed on the following page will include details of adoption or sponsorship programmes. You won't become the legal owner of a kiwi, but your money will help provide food, medical care and attention for kiwi in sanctuaries such as the Otorohanga Kiwi House or the West Coast Wildlife Centre.

When a pure white kiwi hatched at Pukaha Mount Bruce National Wildlife Centre on 1 May 2011, there was a real reason to celebrate. She was a delightful genetic miracle – not an albino, but the offspring of two parents who carried the recessive white feather gene. As the first white kiwi in the world to hatch in captivity, she became a darling of the international press. Local iwi considered her a taonga and named her Manukura, which means 'of chiefly status'.

Later, Manukura experienced a health scare when she swallowed a stone that was too big to move through her system in the normal way and had to be removed. The procedure was performed by a noted Wellington urologist, Rod Studd, and filmed by international media. Manukura recovered well and is now home in her kiwi house. Her caregivers at Pukaha Mount Bruce are raising money to buy special cameras that will allow visitors to watch her even when she is in her burrow. For details of how you can donate to the cause, visit: www.pukaha.org.nz/make-a-donation

12. Where can you see captive kiwi?

Visit any of the places listed here:

North Island

- Kiwi North, Whangarei, www.kiwinorth.co.nz
- Auckland Zoo, Auckland, www.aucklandzoo.co.nz
- Kiwi Encounter at Rainbow Springs, Rotorua, rainbowsprings.co.nz
- Te Puia, the New Zealand Māori Arts and Craft Institute, Rotorua, www.tepuia.com
- Kiwi House and Native Bird Park, Otorohanga, www.kiwihouse.org.nz
- National Aquarium of New Zealand, Napier, www.nationalaquarium.co.nz
- Nga Manu Trust, Waikanae, www.ngamanu.co.nz
- Pukaha, Mount Bruce National Wildlife Centre, Wairarapa, www.pukaha.org.nz
- Wellington Zoo, Wellington, www.wellingtonzoo.com

South Island

- Orana Wildlife Park, Christchurch, www.oranawildlifepark.co.nz
- Willowbank Wildlife Reserve, Christchurch, www.willowbank.co.nz
- Kiwi Birdlife Park, Queenstown, www.kiwibird.co.nz
- National Kiwi Centre, Hokitika, www.thenationalkiwicentre.co.nz
- West Coast Wildlife Centre, Franz Josef, www.wildkiwi.co.nz

How to be an eco-conscious Kiwi

Growing numbers of Kiwis are discovering the feel-good factor that comes from volunteering with a community conservation group. Conservation projects focus on many issues and on many different native flora and fauna – including, of course, the kiwi!

Such projects attract individuals, families, international visitors, students and employees of companies with a community service orientation. Here are some groups that welcome volunteers for various projects in different regions. Some coordinate activities nationwide; others are specific to a particular area.

- 350 Aotearoa, http://350.org.nz – online campaigns, grassroots organising and mass public actions to reduce the amount of CO_2 in the atmosphere to below 350 parts per million

- Ark in the Park, www.arkinthepark.org.nz – bait line maintenance, trap checking, bird monitoring, weed removal, track maintenance and planting in Auckland's Waitakere Ranges Regional Park

- Conservation Volunteers, www.conservationvolunteers.co.nz – track construction and maintenance, interpretive signage, fencing, weed and pest control, revegetation activities

- CUE Haven, http://cuehaven.com – planting out a 24-hectare farm near the Kaipara Harbour in Northland to turn it back into native forest and to create a safe haven for native birds

- Department of Conservation, www.doc.govt.nz – bird counts, historic building restoration, habitat restoration, hut maintenance, weed control, whale strandings, tree planting

- Forest & Bird, www.forestandbird.org.nz – tree planting, bird population monitoring, pest control

- Project Jonah, www.projectjonah.org.nz – assisting at whale stranding emergencies and beach clean-ups.

Who was the Goodnight Kiwi?

The Goodnight Kiwi and his friend the cat first appeared on our TV screens in 1975, a year after the introduction of colour TV – and TV2, our second channel. The Goodnight Kiwi would come out when the evening's viewing was over. As he left the studio, he'd flick off the lights, put the milk bottle out, and race the cat upstairs to a satellite dish where his bed was located. As the strains of the traditional Māori lullaby 'Hine, e Hine' drew to a close, he would gaze out benevolently over Television Land before tucking himself into bed under a thick blue-and-white checked quilt with the cat snuggling in beside him. Here it is on YouTube: www.youtube.com/watch?v=2H2BOGGUbm4

A kiwi glossary

Instant Kiwi the nation in a nutshell; a lottery ticket

Kiwi (informal) a New Zealander

kiwi a flightless nocturnal bird with bristly feathers, a long bill and no tail; also, what the rest of the world calls kiwifruit

Kiwi Concert Party a wartime entertainment troupe that performed for New Zealand soldiers in the field

Kiwi Country an informal name for New Zealand

Kiwi Ferns the New Zealand international women's rugby league team

Kiwi green locally grown cannabis

Kiwi House informal name for New Zealand House in London

Kiwi ingenuity the much revered ability of New Zealanders who manage to find creative solutions to practical problems, even under difficult circumstances

Kiwi Keith Keith Holyoake, prime minister of New Zealand 1960–72

Kiwi shoe polish long-serving and internationally popular boot polish, invented by an Australian

kiwi zone an area managed as a sanctuary for kiwi

kiwiana items and artefacts that represent quintessential New Zealand

Kiwiana Town Otorohanga, in the Waikato, the official home of kiwiana

Kiwibank a trading bank set up by the government in 2002

Kiwiburger	the brainchild of McDonald's franchisee Bryan Old, who lobbied for permission to sell a hamburger with the classic New Zealand ingredients of sliced beetroot and a fried egg
kiwifruit	a small fruit with green or gold flesh and brown furry skin, formerly known as 'Chinese gooseberry'
kiwify	to imbue something with a New Zealand character
KiwiSaver	a retirement savings scheme introduced in 2007
Kiwispeak	New Zealand English
the Kiwi	the New Zealand dollar
the Kiwis	the New Zealand international men's rugby league team
New Kiwis	a website, www.newkiwis.co.nz, that links skilled migrants with potential New Zealand employers

Chapter seven

A YEAR IN THE LIFE OF NEW ZEALAND

A Kiwi community calendar

To get to grips with the inimitable Kiwi psyche, fill your diary along the lines of the following calendar, and you'll soon end up with a sense of our special style.

MONTH	TO SEE KIWIS WHO ARE …	PLAN A: THE KEY EVENT	PLAN B: THE ALTERNATIVE(S)
January	Keen to make the most of the summer sunshine	Ports of Auckland Anniversary Day Regatta	• International cricket and tennis • Karaka Million horse race
February	Not afraid of gut-busting physical challenges	Speight's Coast to Coast	• Golden Shears shearing championship • Mission Estate Winery Concert
March	Proud of our South Pacific connections	Pasifika Festival	• Wildfoods Festival • Te Houtaewa Challenge epic beach race
April	Unapologetically unpretentious	Running of the Sheep	• Middlemarch Singles Ball • Warbirds Over Wanaka

May	Lovers of good food and fun	Bluff Oyster & Food Festival	• Firefighters Sky Tower Stair Challenge • New Zealand Gold Guitar Awards
June	Ingeniously artistic	No. 8 Wire Art Awards and Fieldays	• American Express Queenstown Winter Festival • Nude rugby
July	Awesome agricultural types	ANZ Young Farmer Contest	• Cadbury Jaffa Race
August	Up for an adrenaline rush	World Heli Challenge	• Bledisloe Cup rugby
September	At the cutting edge of creativity	World of WearableArt Awards Show	• Wayleggo Cup sheepdog trials
October	Certain of their priorities	Speight's Perfect Woman	• Armageddon Expo
November	Willing to put in the hard yards for charity	Contact Lake Taupo Cycle Challenge	• Canterbury A&P Show • Farmers Santa Parade
December	Family-oriented	Coca-Cola Christmas in the Park	• Rhythm and Vines

Worth a look: the events in detail

JANUARY

Ports of Auckland Anniversary Day Regatta

Held every year except one since 1850, this is when Waitemata Harbour fills with several hundred vessels: tall ships, sloops, multihulls, dragonboats, powerboats, vintage tugboats, yachts and Māori waka. For the sake of tradition, find a good picnic spot – maybe on North Head or Tamaki Drive – and settle down to watch the day's racing. View the programme at: www.regatta.org.nz

Sport support

Limitless hours can be devoted to armchair cricket, especially during visits from international sides such as India, the West Indies or Sri Lanka. For cricket news and schedules, visit: www.blackcaps.co.nz

Anyone for tennis? Two weeks of international competition, held annually in Auckland in the first two weeks of January, attracts some top seeds and provides a warm-up for the Australian Open. For information, check: www.tennisnz.com

New Zealand Bloodstock Karaka Million

In January, hundreds of fine-bred one-year-old horses are sold under the hammer at the National Yearling Sales in Karaka. The evening before, the country's richest horse race is run over 1200 metres in front of the industry's top owners, trainers, breeders and buyers. Find more information about race events at: www.nzracing.co.nz

FEBRUARY

Speight's Coast to Coast
You don't have to be an elite athlete to enter the Speight's Coast to Coast, but it would help. Up to 800 competitors stagger from one side of the country to the other by cycling 140 kilometres, running 36 kilometres (including 33 kilometres across the Southern Alps) and kayaking 67 kilometres through the Waimakariri Gorge. If you insist on entering, visit www.coasttocoast.co.nz first, and follow the '9 Steps for Newbies' training programme.

Mission Estate Winery Concert
At the Mission Estate, the oldest winery in Hawke's Bay, top-class acts are brought in to entertain while visitors enjoy a picnic on the grass and plenty of good wine. In 1993 Dame Kiri Te Kanawa appeared, and since then the Mission Estate has attracted the likes of Rod Stewart, Eric Clapton, Carole King, Ray Charles, the Beach Boys and the Doobie Brothers. For information, check out: www.missionestate.co.nz/events/annual_mission_concert

Golden Shears
The annual Golden Shears shearing and wool handling championship held in Masterton is a Kiwi institution. In the stifling heat of the woolshed, shearers work at speed, dragging the sheep from their pens, flipping them on their backs, and deftly relieving them of their heavy fleeces without damaging the wool, the sheep or themselves. Shearer David Fagan has won the Golden Shears 16 times and still competes internationally. To watch him shear a sheep in 14 seconds, visit: www.youtube.com/watch?v=TbUDbH6tjGs

MARCH

Pasifika Festival
For two days, around 225,000 visitors descend on Western Springs in Auckland to circulate among 'villages' that showcase the art, craft and food of 11 Pacific Island communities. Captivating displays of dancing and drumming are staged on both days, and a multidenominational church service is held on the Sunday morning with the theme of 'many nations, one god'. See: www.aucklandnz.com/pasifika

Wildfoods Festival
Each March, the small West Coast town of Hokitika stages a Wildfoods Festival. Tummy rumbling for a grasshopper, sheep's testicle or chocolate-covered huhu beetle? If not, we can recommend the scallop kebabs, wild pork sausages and whitebait fritters. Don't forget to save room for the wasp-larvae ice cream to follow. See: www.wildfoods.co.nz

Te Houtaewa Challenge
At Ninety Mile Beach, local iwi host a marathon with an interesting cultural precedent. The event honours Te Houtaewa, the speediest sprinter of his day, who managed to outrun his enemies as they chased him the length of Ninety Mile Beach (which, in fact, has a true length of 55 miles, or 88 kilometres). To read the legend of Te Houtaewa, visit: www.tehoutaewa.co.nz

APRIL

Running of the Sheep
The Great NZ Muster is held on the weekend after Easter in the small Waikato town of Te Kuiti. The climax of the event is the Running of the Sheep, when over 1000 Romneys hoof it down the main street in a woolly version of Pamplona's

Running of the Bulls. A $1000 prize is awarded for correctly guessing the number of sheep. A one-minute video clip of the run is available at: www.youtube.com/watch?v=Rilhu-F7UOU

Middlemarch Singles Ball
Why be lonely just because you live in a tiny town of 300 inhabitants that suffers from a serious shortage of women? That was the thinking that launched the biennial Middlemarch Singles Ball in Central Otago, held at Easter in odd-numbered years since 2001. As local boys polish up their glad rags and gumboots, women arrive on the 'Love Train' from Dunedin, hoping to meet an eligible sheep farmer who will steal their heart.
See: www.middlemarch.co.nz/events/singles-ball.html

Warbirds Over Wanaka
During Easter weekend in even-numbered years, roads are closed, traffic is detoured and necks crane skywards for Warbirds Over Wanaka: a stunning collection of aircraft ranging from historic fighter planes to contemporary jets. The sight of Spitfires overhead has been known to make grown men cry. For the finale, the show erupts into a huge staged air battle, complete with pyrotechnics.
See: www.warbirdsoverwanaka.com

MAY

Bluff Oyster & Food Festival
Each year, the seaside town of Bluff celebrates the start of the oyster season. The festivities get under way with 'piping in the oyster', and there are competitions for oyster opening and eating. For those who prefer to enjoy their seafood delicacies at a non-competitive rate, oysters are prepared and served every possible way, from raw to deep-fried in batter. Around 30,000 are consumed during the one-day event. See: www.bluffoysterfest.co.nz

LOCAL KNOWLEDGE

Oysters down and up

The record for eating oysters is held by former All Black Andy Haden. Andy was in Bluff to help the local rugby club celebrate their centennial in 1989. It was June, oysters were in season, and Andy took up the challenge of the oyster-eating competition. He did very well – for a while; he managed to pack in 222 oysters before, as one journalist reported, his 'sense of wellness deserted him'. Nevertheless, in appreciation of his efforts, Andy was made an honorary citizen of Bluff, and his record stands unbeaten.

Firefighter Sky Tower Stair Challenge

Each May, around 500 firefighters run up the 51 flights of stairs – or 1103 steps – inside Auckland's Sky Tower, wearing their full kit and carrying 25 kilograms of breathing apparatus on their backs. The race calls for spectacular stamina, and contestants are often close to collapse as they finish. The fastest time recorded is 8 minutes and 37 seconds. See: firefightersclimb.org.nz

New Zealand Gold Guitar Awards

Without country music, what balm would there be for a broken heart? Every year for the last 40 years, Gore (New Zealand's answer to Nashville) has got out the banjos, steel guitars and fiddles for a week of country music celebrations, awards, concerts, competitions and inductions into the Hands of Fame. See: www.goldguitars.co.nz

JUNE

No. 8 Wire National Art Award

To the Kiwi mind, No. 8 fencing wire symbolises ingenuity and creativity, because if it couldn't be fixed with a bit of No. 8 wire, it probably was unfixable. That ingenuity is elevated to art form for the No. 8 Wire National Art Award, sponsored by National Agricultural Fieldays, a showcase of cutting-edge agricultural technology held each year at Mystery Creek. To view the wiry artworks, go to: www.fieldays.co.nz/no8wire

Nude rugby match

In 2002, the Irish were in Dunedin to play the All Blacks. Before the test match, local students took on some visiting backpackers in a rugby match on the beach at St Clair. Both teams played stark naked, refusing to let anything stand in the way of a good game. Since then, the fixture has been held before any international test match played in Dunedin (usually one a year), and up to 2000 stand on the sidelines to observe the somewhat unedifying spectacle. Brace yourself to catch the nude rugby on: www.rugbydump.com/2013/10/3451/the-nude-blacks-get-the-better-of-their-australian-counterparts-in-annual-match

American Express Queenstown Winter Festival

Also described as 'New Zealand's Ten Coolest Days', the Queenstown Winter Festival is basically a big winter party. Up on Coronet Peak, the snow is negotiated at breakneck speed as contestants hurtle down the slopes on a mountain bike, slide down in an open suitcase or run down with a faithful canine companion at heel. On Lake Wakatipu, there's a birdman competition in which one ambitious pilot after another attempts to fly some strange contraption out over the frigid waters. See: www.winterfestival.co.nz

JULY

ANZ Young Farmer Contest – Grand Finals
This annual contest reassures us that our nation's economy is in the hands of people who can not only shear sheep, build fences and assemble farm equipment, but run a multimillion dollar enterprise as well. Two days of gruelling contest climaxes in a live televised quiz show, with over $300,000 in prizes up for grabs. See: www.youngfarmercontest.co.nz

Cadbury Jaffa Race
The highlight of Dunedin's Cadbury Chocolate Carnival is the Jaffa Race. Conducted on Baldwin Street – recognised by Guinness World Records as the steepest street in the world – the race involves releasing a tidal wave of 25,000 individually numbered Jaffas (chocolate balls with an orange candy coating) at the top of the street and watching them bounce their way to the bottom. See: www.chocolatecarnival.co.nz/jaffa_race

AUGUST

World Heli Challenge
Selected skiers and snowboarders from around the world demonstrate their snowmanship in the Southern Alps surrounding Wanaka. After being dropped off by helicopter on the summit of a back-country mountain, contestants make a hard and fearless descent, using acrobatic and aerial skills to exploit the steep slopes and vertical precipices. Video footage of their daring is available at: www.worldhelichallenge.com

Bledisloe Cup rugby
Want to the see the Wallabies get beaten? Each year, our own All Blacks clash with the Australian national rugby team in a series of three encounters starting

in August. At stake is the highly coveted Bledisloe Cup, which the All Blacks have a history of winning for decades at a time. Despite our long-held grip on the trophy, we are charitable enough to say that the outcome is never certain. For details of venues and dates, check: www.allblacks.com

SEPTEMBER

World of WearableArt
A show that began in Nelson over 20 years ago as a novelty event for local designers has grown into a global phenomenon. The World of WearableArt is not just about clothing items that are works of art; it's more about works of art that require a human form to bring them to life and propel them around a stage in an extravagant display of colour, form and dance. The event has moved to Wellington, and brings together more than 300 designers for a week of avant-garde theatricality. See: www.worldofwearableart.com

Wayleggo Cup
'Wayleggo' is shorthand for 'come away and let go', a command shouted by shepherds to their dogs as they work in tandem to control the movement of stock. The Wayleggo Cup is awarded to the winners of trans-Tasman sheep dog trials, in which dogs must respond to their master's instructions and guide sheep through four obstacles – a gate, a Maltese cross, a ramp and a pen – before the 15-minute time limit is reached. For details of other sheepdog trials, visit: www.sheepdogtrials.co.nz

OCTOBER

Speight's Perfect Woman
Is this competition degrading to women? Hardly. Winning has nothing to do with good looks and everything to do with competence. It judges contestants'

ability to open a bottle of beer without an opener, sling a goat carcass onto your back, change a tyre, skin a possum, dig in a fence post, play a respectable game of pool, give a resounding blast on a dog whistle and reverse a trailer loaded with hay. All in a day's work, apparently, for the perfect woman. To understand the competition's advertising origins, look at: www.youtube.com/watch?v=LAVMYGwOqmA

Armageddon Expo

Kiwi workers have been celebrating their achievement of an 8-hour day since 1890, but the huge street parades and the respectful shutting of shops are a thing of the past. Labour Day weekend is still an October holiday, but it's now noted for the celebration of leisure time in formats unthinkable in earlier times. Armageddon, the country's largest annual expo, is a nerd-fest, a gaming haven, where showgoers often dress as zombies or other frightful characters. See: www.armageddonexpo.com/nz

NOVEMBER

Contact Lake Taupo Cycle Challenge

Up to 10,000 riders mount their bikes and pedal off around Lake Taupo in New Zealand's largest cycling event, raising funds for children with heart problems. One lap of the lake is a distance of 160 kilometres, and while the best can cover it in under 4.5 hours, others may not cross the finishing line until 12 hours have elapsed. It doesn't matter; maybe the slower riders stop to enjoy the spectacular views. Full inspiration is online at: www.cyclechallenge.com

Canterbury A&P Show

The Agricultural and Pastoral (A&P) Show is a revered tradition in Canterbury, and sufficient reason for a public holiday. During a packed three-day programme of sheep-shearing contests, horse and pony events, woodchopping displays and dog trials, over 3000 animals compete for showing titles. The Supreme Champion Animal of the Show has the honour of leading the prizewinners behind the Caledonian Pipe Band for the Ballantynes Grand Parade. See: www.theshow.co.nz

Farmers Santa Parade

Farmers, in this case, refers to the century-old department store, not to blokes in black singlets, shorts and gumboots. The Farmers Santa Parade through Auckland's CBD has been a family favourite for 80 years. A stream of floats and strolling cartoon characters meander along the 2.2-kilometre route until the climactic moment when old Saint Nick makes his appearance on his sleigh, heroically smiling and waving despite being unseasonably dressed for the hot summer sun. See: www.santaparade.co.nz

DECEMBER

Coca-Cola Christmas in the Park

In both Auckland and Christchurch, families take their blankets and chillybins and settle in for an evening of Christmas music entertainment under the (hopefully) starry skies. Despite huge crowds, the mood is relaxed, the entertainment keeps rolling, and volunteers circulate with buckets to collect donations on behalf of Surf Life Saving New Zealand. Details are at: www.christmasinthepark.co.nz

Rhythm and Vines

Gisborne is the place to rock out the year's end with a little 'background' music: an eardrum-challenging three-day line-up of music called Rhythm and Vines. If you can't bear to tear yourself away each night, you can camp onsite at the festival. Information is available at: www.rhythmandvines.co.nz

LOCAL KNOWLEDGE

Quintessential Kiwi summer living

January is beach and barbecue time, a chance to recover from the excesses of the festive season before heading back to work and school later in the month – sometimes with the annoying realisation that the steadiest spells of warm, sunny weather often occur in February. Nevertheless, as soon as the Christmas holidays start, Kiwis optimistically install themselves in beachside baches, tents, motorhomes and caravans and are fairly regularly forced to evacuate their campground because a cyclone has beaten a path down from the Pacific Islands. While the sun shines, though, 'casual' is key: neighbours are invited around to help eat up the leftover ham or turkey, or simply to share a few sausages and some salad and a nice cold beer, before the New Year's diet starts in earnest.

Untouchable girls

The Topp Twins are twin sisters, musicians, political activists, a comedy duo . . . and a cultural institution. We were chuffed when, on 20 September 2009, *The Topp Twins: Untouchable Girls* scooped the People's Choice Award, Best Documentary, at the Toronto International Film Festival. We knew then that the rest of the world shared our love for Jools and Lynda, whom one film critic described as 'ebullient yodelling lesbian twin-sister farmer songbirds from rural New Zealand'. To us, they're queens of country music who know just how to make us laugh – especially at our own expense.

In our own backyard

New Zealand's *Country Calendar* comes second only to *Coronation Street* as the world's longest-running TV programme. In 1966 it went to air for the first time, with a less-than-riveting report on market prices and an interview with the chairman of the Meat Board, shot in the studio with the presenter and interviewee wearing suits and ties. These days, camera crews head into the country, putting farmers centre stage and supplementing traditional topics with not-so-predictable items: following an episode on sheep mustering in the high country might be a profile of horse breakers, truffle growers, eel farmers or organic brewers. Few shows have such instantly identifiable and catchy theme music: in this case, it's 'Hillbilly Child' by Alan Moorhouse. Within the first three notes, Kiwis know it's time to take their place on the couch. You can hear it at: www.youtube.com/watch?v=jqmpVrgho6g

A five-part retrospective that revisits highlights from the first 40 years of *Country Calendar* can be found at:
www.nzonscreen.com/title/40-years-of-country-calendar-2005

Chapter eight

MADE IN NEW ZEALAND

KIWI IDEAS THAT HAVE MADE
THE WORLD A BETTER PLACE

Kiwi ideas that have made the world a better place

A safe trampoline

Keith Alexander invented the world's safest trampoline, now found in gardens all over New Zealand and around the world. His design replaces the traditional steel coil springs with glass-reinforced rods, an innovation that is said to reduce accidents and injuries by up to 80 percent.

A whistle for the ref

In June 1884, William Atack became the first referee in the world to use a whistle to stop a game. It was logistical brilliance because, until then, referees had to raise their voices to control games, which was exhausting when you had to shout over two competing teams. Now used universally.

Affordable medical treatment

Ray Avery founded the development agency Medicine Mondiale, a network of scientific, clinical and business experts who volunteer time and knowledge to develop medical solutions that improve health care on a global scale.

Kiwifruit creations

Jan Bilton revealed the culinary personality of the kiwifruit to an international audience through her *New Zealand Kiwifruit Cookbook*. When publishers rejected her initial proposal for the book, she published it herself in April 1981 and sold 10,000 copies in the first month. It is now in its fourth edition and has sold over 140,000 copies internationally.

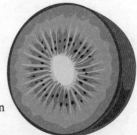

Precision electromagnets

Bill Buckley's technology company is the world's leading supplier of precision electromagnets. The electromagnets are used in the manufacture of 90 percent of the world's silicon chips – leaving Buckley's professional stamp on probably every much-cherished computer, smartphone and other digital gizmo in your personal collection.

The Mountain Buggy

Allan Croad revolutionised infant transport in 1992 when he designed the Mountain Buggy, an all-terrain pushchair that is light, strong and very manoeuvrable.

Iconic Kiwi décor

Fred and Myrtle Flutey elevated pāua shells to the level of décor icon by covering almost every last centimetre of their home in Bluff with Fred's prized collection of 1170 polished shells. The turquoise-painted home became a quirky museum and Fred and Myrtle would receive around 25,000 visitors each year. After their deaths, the Flutey home was reconstructed in the Canterbury Museum.

The electric fence

Irritated by witnessing his old horse Joe regularly scratch his rump on the family car, Bill Gallagher responded by developing the electric fence, now used by farmers around the world to keep stock contained.

A leap of faith

A. J. Hackett created the bungy (a system of plaited elastic bands) and, at the Eiffel Tower in 1987, demonstrated the adrenaline rush to be gained from tying one around your ankles and leaping from a great height. Now, each year, more than 100,000 visitors to New Zealand take the plunge at various leaping-off points around the country.

The jetboat
Bill Hamilton invented the world's first jetboat in 1953; it can be operated in shallow water without the fear of striking rocks. He also has to his credit a machine that smoothes ice on skating rinks.

The rotary milking platform
Merv Hicks, a Taranaki farmer, invented the rotary milking platform in the late 1960s. The turnstile design consists of a circular platform with between 16 and 60 stalls. As it rotates, cows walk on and are milked by operators standing on the circumference of the platform. Cows back themselves off once the milking cups are removed.

Schools and hospitals for the Sherpa people
Ed Hillary used the fame created by his ascent of Mount Everest in 1953 to raise funds for development projects that benefited the Sherpa people of Nepal, such as the building of schools and hospitals.

Sight for the blind
Ophthalmologist Fred Hollows visited countries like Nepal, Eritrea and Vietnam, training doctors in eyesight-restoring surgical procedures for those unable to afford good health care. It has been estimated that more than a million people can see today because of the work done by his Foundation.

Movies from magical mythology
Peter Jackson has fired the imaginations of millions around the world and boosted New Zealand's profile as a filming location with his movie adaptations of J. R. R. Tolkien's *The Lord of the Rings* and *The Hobbit*.

A careful catch
Scientist Alistair Jerrett developed a fish-trawling technique called 'Precision

Seafood Harvesting'. Instead of the traditional mesh trawling net, it uses a large, tube-shaped PVC liner to catch a specific species of fish while allowing other species – and undersized fish – to escape. Regarded as the biggest advance for the fishing industry in 150 years, the programme was introduced in 2013.

Caring for mother and baby
Truby King established the Plunket Society in 1907 to help mothers and babies who were suffering from malnutrition and disease. Plunket still promotes the wellbeing of mothers and babies, and advocates strongly for children's rights. King was the first private citizen in New Zealand to be given a state funeral.

Politics with a conscience
Norman Kirk, the 29th prime minister of New Zealand, withdrew Kiwi troops from Vietnam, sent two navy frigates into the Pacific to protest French nuclear testing, and refused to allow a visit by a South African rugby team as a protest gesture against the policy of apartheid.

A class act
Lorde – real name Ella Marija Lani Yelich-O'Connor – is an Auckland teenage singer-songwriter and the first Kiwi to hit number one on the US Billboard charts. Apart from her winning two Grammy awards in February 2014, we love her for her anti-consumerist ideals, and because she doesn't poke her tongue out or twerk, like some of her northern hemisphere counterparts.

Jogging
Arthur Lydiard invented jogging as a way of building physical fitness by gradually increasing stamina. His training techniques guided his protégés Peter Snell and Murray Halberg to gold on the same day at the 1960 Rome Olympics.

Humble humour
The comedy and music of Bret McKenzie and Jemaine Clement, aka Flight of the Conchords, became the basis of an American TV series, and in September 2010 they guest starred as a pair of camp counsellors in 'Elementary School Musical', the season premiere of the 22nd season of *The Simpsons*.

Brilliant books for children
Margaret Mahy wrote more than 100 delightful picture books, 40 novels and 20 collections of short stories. She won the Hans Christian Andersen Award for her lasting contribution to children's literature worldwide.

A flying machine
Glenn Martin developed the Martin Jetpack, which will keep you aloft for over 30 minutes at a speed of up to 74 kilometres per hour and altitudes above 800 feet. The Jetpack was developed initially for the first-responder community but is now being developed for leisure and personal use.

The disposable syringe
Colin Murdoch came up with the idea of a disposable syringe as a way of eliminating the risk, associated with glass syringes, of transmitting disease from animal to animal or person to person. When he first presented his plastic syringe to the New Zealand Health Department, his idea was rejected as 'too futuristic'. Now, every year, over 16 billion plastic syringes are used worldwide.

Spreadable butter
Robert Norris and David Illingworth developed spreadable butter, which meant that we no longer had to resort to margarine if we wanted to avoid ripping holes in the bread. All butter is made with cream and salt; the secret to spreadable butter is to physically remove those parts of the cream that make ordinary butter too hard to spread at fridge temperature.

Seismic shock absorbers

Bill Robinson invented the base isolators that keep buildings and bridges stable in even the strongest earthquake. In Los Angeles on 17 January 1994, several hospitals in the Northridge area were affected by an earthquake measuring 6.7 on the Richter scale, but one hospital continued to function throughout – the one protected by Robinson's base isolators.

Nuclear physics

Ernest Rutherford is credited with 'splitting' the atom. His biographer, John Campbell, a physicist at the University of Canterbury, says Rutherford is to the atom 'what Darwin is to evolution, Newton to mechanics, Faraday to electricity and Einstein to relativity'. Rutherford was described by Einstein as 'the man who tunnelled into the very material of God'.

Protecting nature

Guy Salmon led the native forest conservation movement from 1975, which culminated in the establishment of the Department of Conservation in 1987. He now advises governments on climate change, water management, electricity markets, fisheries, forestry, land transport and overseas development assistance.

Fine romance

Essie Summers provided essential reading for lovers of pulp romance. By the time she died in 1998, aged 86, she'd written more than 50 novels for Mills and Boon, and was known as New Zealand's Queen of Romance.

Improved armchair sports

Ian Taylor founded a computer animation company that produces award-winning sports graphics. His product, Virtual Spectator, is used in various sports – for example, for ball-tracking in cricket – to help umpires make good decisions; it also helps spectators understand what they are watching.

Chapter nine

THE KIWI INDEX

A KIWI COLLECTION OF CURIOUS FACTS
AND ODDBALL STATS

LOCAL KNOWLEDGE:
SPOILED FOR CHOICE: TWO NATIONAL ANTHEMS

AOTEAROA GOD DEFEND NEW ZEALAND

A Kiwi collection of curious facts and oddball stats

4.5 MILLION	Population of New Zealand. (Watch the population clock ticking at: www.stats.govt.nz)
100	Number of New Zealanders turning 50 every day
3	Official languages of New Zealand: English, Māori, New Zealand Sign Language
5.18	Number of Australians for every New Zealander
7	Number of sheep for every New Zealander. (In 1982, there were 22 sheep for every person)
0	Number of foreign invasions of New Zealand
2.4 MILLION	Number of viewers of the TV One news special that covered the Canterbury earthquake on 22 February 2011. (In comparison, 2.2 million viewers watched the marriage of Prince William and Kate Middleton)
80,000	Kiwis out of the country on short overseas trips on any given day
2.5 MILLION	People who 'like' the All Blacks on Facebook (and growing every hour)
28	The average age for first-time Kiwi mums
213	Claims related to jandals made to the Accident Compensation Corporation in 2013
1.7	Laps of the coastline of New Zealand to equal one lap around Australia

27	Air New Zealand domestic destinations
73	Percentage of dead New Zealanders who are cremated
18	Number of meat pies the average Kiwi eats each year
$36.9 MILLION	The largest individual NZ Lotteries prize, won in 2009 by a syndicate of four family members from Masterton
613,000	Gigalitres of rainfall on New Zealand in 2010, enough to fill Lake Taupo more than 10 times
65	Percentage of Kiwis who live within 5km of the coast
41	New Zealand-bred horses that have won the Melbourne Cup
35	Number of hours Lydia Ko practised golf each week – even before turning professional
13	Megatonnes of methane emitted by cattle and sheep each year in New Zealand
81.3	Weight (in kg) of the average Kiwi adult (just a little lighter than the average American, who weighs 82.7kg)
26	Items banned from sale on Trade Me auction website – including menacing dogs, tobacco, and human body parts
726,656	Pairs of gumboots imported in 2012
692	Wineries in New Zealand in 2013
44	Unprovoked shark attacks recorded in New Zealand since 1852
5	New Zealand prime ministers whose first and last names together total 10 letters: Walter Nash, Joseph Ward, Norman Kirk, David Lange, Helen Clark
1 BILLION	Approximate number of eggs laid by New Zealand's 3.2 million hens each year

89	Percentage of New Zealand enterprises with five or fewer employees
483	Weight (in kg) of the biggest fish caught in New Zealand: a 5m long marlin, caught on 16 April 2009
6235	Licensed pink-coloured cars in New Zealand in 2012
32	Warmest Christmas Day temperature (in °C) ever in New Zealand, recorded in Dunedin in 2009
53,256,697	Issues from New Zealand public libraries for the 2011/12 year
10	Visits by Queen Elizabeth II to New Zealand
11	Films banned by the censor for viewing in New Zealand
93.7	Percentage of the population that voted in the General Election on 14 July 1984 – the highest voter turnout in New Zealand's history
$7.7 BILLION	Value of total imports from China in 2012
67	Species that have become extinct in New Zealand since humans arrived
26,770	Registered charities in New Zealand
38	UFO sightings reported in 2013
125,352	Māori who could hold a conversation in te reo Māori in 2013 (21.3 percent of Māori)
8.2	The strongest earthquake recorded in New Zealand. It occurred in the Wairarapa, in 1855.
$52	Average value of an electronic card transaction in 2013
1, 7 AND 13	The three most commonly drawn Lotto numbers
4	Stars on the New Zealand flag representing the Southern Cross

The Kiwi ABC: an iconic alphabet

A is for Anzac Day

On 25 April each year, more and more Kiwis willingly stumble out of bed to attend dawn ceremonies to honour those who died fighting in wars overseas. Particularly remembered are those 2721 young soldiers who died during a 9-month campaign against Turkish opponents at Gallipoli in 1915. Their courage and sacrifice under appalling conditions is regarded as the catalyst that forged a uniquely Kiwi sense of identity.

B is for 'Bring Back Buck'

Don't be surprised if at any gathering of Kiwi sports lovers you see a sign held up somewhere in the crowd that reads 'Bring Back Buck'. Wayne 'Buck' Shelford captained the All Blacks from 1987 to 1990. During that time, the All Blacks won all their matches except for one draw. When Shelford was dumped from the team in 1990, there was a huge outcry. Despite calls to radio, letters to newspapers, and a proliferation of 'Bring Back Buck' signs at sportsgrounds, the selectors remained unmoved, but their decision is still decried today.

C is for cable car

Wellington's bright red cable cars have been sliding up and down their tracks between Lambton Quay in the CBD and the top entrance of the Botanic Gardens (and one of the best views over Wellington) since 1902. Although the distance is obviously the same, the fare for going uphill is $4 and downhill is $3.50. Along the way there are three stops, including one for the Kelburn campus of Victoria University. In 1926 some 2 million people were transported – more than the population of New Zealand at that time.

D is for dairies
Small convenience stores often located on a street corner, dairies sell everything from magazines and milk to lottery tickets and loo paper.

E is for *Edmonds Cookery Book*
The *Edmonds Cookery Book* has sold over 3.45 million copies since it was first published in 1908, making it this country's best-selling book by a country mile. What started as a promotional tool for the Edmonds brand of baking powder has become the recipe bible for most New Zealand homes. It contains recipes for many unpretentious Kiwi favourites, such as bacon and egg pie and pikelets.

F is for fish and chips, a fast food favourite
Despite stiff competition from Asian takeaways, fish and chips is still one of the country's favourite fast foods – best eaten on the beach, or in front of the TV on a Friday night. There are industry standards for those who deep-fry the food for us, including the 'bang and hang' guideline: 'After frying, bang or shake the basket vigorously two times. Then hang the basket for at least 20 seconds.' Check www.chipgroup.co.nz for a list of winning outlets in the annual Best Chip Shop competition.

G is for Goldie
Charles Frederick Goldie was a 19th-century artist whose portraits of Māori dignitaries now fetch fabulous prices. When opera diva Kiri Te Kanawa offered *Forty Winks, a portrait of Rutene Te Uamairangi* for sale in November 2010, it reached $573,000, the most ever paid for a painting at auction in New Zealand at that time. More recently, in November 2013, a Goldie portrait of Kawhena (also known as Johnny Coffin) was sold at auction for $733,000.

H is for heitiki
The heitiki – more commonly called the 'tiki' – is a carved greenstone or

bone ornament worn around the neck. A few decades ago, Air New Zealand would issue a plastic version to each passenger, sealed in cellophane, together with a tiny booklet. The practice stopped when heitiki began to be widely acknowledged as taonga (treasured possessions) that didn't deserve such insensitive commercial exploitation.

I is for the Interislander
The ferry that crosses Cook Strait between Wellington and Picton. The 92-kilometre voyage takes three hours. On a good day, it can be one of the most beautiful ferry rides in the world; during rough weather, bilious passengers would rather be anywhere else on earth.

J is for jandals
An abbreviation of 'Japanese' and 'sandals', jandals are the favourite rubber footwear of casual Kiwis. The country's Surf Life Saving association runs an annual fundraising appeal in December called National Jandal Day, when everyone is encouraged to wear their jandals and donate generously to help lifesavers save lives on New Zealand's beaches.

K is for kiwiana
'Kiwiana' is the group name for all those objects and items we regard as representing quintessential New Zealand. For full immersion in the concept of kiwiana, head to Otorohanga, in southern Waikato farm country, just over 50 kilometres from Hamilton. This small, friendly town has been officially declared (by then prime minister Helen Clark) the country's Kiwiana Town, for its celebration of all Kiwi classics, from the Buzzy Bee, pāua and pavlova to Ed Hillary, the haka and hokey pokey ice cream. For a full explanation, visit: www.kiwianatown.co.nz.

L is for *The Lord of the Rings*

Directed by Peter Jackson, this trilogy – filmed entirely in New Zealand – went on to win a staggering haul of 17 Oscars. Matamata is home to the Hobbiton movie set, a spin-off attraction. For a list of filming locations, visit: www.newzealand.com/int/feature/lord-of-the-rings

M is for the Māori Battalion

Formed shortly after the outbreak of World War II, the 28th (Māori) Battalion earned a reputation for unbeatable bravery and spirit, particularly during the Western Desert Campaign in North Africa and on the battlefields of Greece, Crete and Italy. See: www.28Maoribattalion.org.nz

N is for Nuclear Free Zone

On 10 July 1985, the Greenpeace protest ship *Rainbow Warrior* was blown up in the Auckland harbour by two French secret agents. Their terrorist action cemented in us a very determined anti-nuclear stance that would be enshrined in Nuclear Free Zone legislation within two years. On 12 December 1987, the *Rainbow Warrior* was scuttled in Matauri Bay in the Bay of Islands and now serves as a dive wreck; visit: www.divetherainbowwarrior.co.nz

O is for Opo

Opo was a young female bottlenose dolphin much beloved by beachgoers at the Northland holiday resort of Opononi during the summer of 1955–56. She became internationally famous for her playful antics and even had a song written about her. A law was passed to protect all dolphins in the Hokianga Harbour where Opo played, but a day after its introduction, Opo died mysteriously. A statue to her memory still stands at Opononi.

P is for pesky possums

Introduced to this country from Australia in the 1830s, possums have become a nationwide pest: they wreak havoc in the bush by chewing through 7 million tonnes of vegetation each year. To rid ourselves of this scourge, we poison them, bait them and shoot them. We even wrap our utility poles in sheet metal to stop possums climbing them. More creatively, these days we turn possum fur into fashion items such as gloves, hats and socks.

Q is for the Queen's Birthday Honours

Even though we sometimes think about becoming a republic, we'd never want to give up the holiday we get to celebrate the Queen's birthday. It takes place on the Monday following the first weekend in June. We also wouldn't want to give up the Queen's Birthday Honours, handed out in recognition of good works and good lives. The highest honour that can be awarded is the Order of New Zealand. Current members of the Order include opera singer Kiri Te Kanawa; filmmaker Peter Jackson; first elected female prime minister Helen Clark; and the Queen's husband, Prince Philip, who was appointed to the Order to mark the Queen's Diamond Jubilee.

R is for rugby

The national religion, some say. Newcomers to New Zealand are well advised to add words like 'ruck', 'maul', 'scrum' and 'lineout' – together with the reproach 'Are ya blind, ref?' – to their vocabulary as soon as possible. We're passionate about the game, and it only takes an All Black win against Australia, South Africa, France or England for the mood of the entire country to lift. (It's best not to be around if we lose.)

S is for Shrek

Among the national flock of 31 million, we found a celebrity. Shrek the sheep lived on Bendigo Station in the South Island, where he evaded capture for six years. When Shrek was eventually caught by musterer Ann Scanlan, the 27-kilogram fleece he had grown while in hiding was shorn under the amused gaze of a worldwide television audience. Shrek became an international star. He featured on TV shows, was the subject of three books, toured the country, met the prime minister, and raised $150,000 for charity before he died at the age of 17 in 2011.

T is for tui

A New Zealand native bird with a distinctive white tuft under its throat. Also, a brand of beer ubiquitously promoted with cheeky billboard advertising that features the cynical slogan 'Yeah, right.' For example, just before Waitangi Day 2008, Tui erected a billboard that said 'Muskets, blankets and beads. Sounds like a fair trade... Yeah, right.'

U is for ultraviolet

Ultraviolet (UV) radiation is especially harsh in New Zealand, because of our clear skies and low levels of air pollution. Because excess exposure increases the risk of developing melanoma (skin cancer), sunbathing is pretty much a no-no. Instead, each summer the nationwide SunSmart programme tells us to 'Slip, Slop, Slap and Wrap': slip on a shirt, slop on the 30+ sunscreen, slap on a hat and wear wraparound sunglasses.

V is for villa

The first mass housing style in New Zealand, the villa is a square-shaped house originally made of native timbers such as rimu, kauri, tōtara and mataī, with a corrugated iron roof. The floorplan is predictable: a series of rooms opening off a large central hall; the kitchen, laundry and bathroom are usually found at the back of the house. A single-bay villa has a bay window on one side and a verandah on the other. The earliest examples of the villa were constructed in the 1880s.

W is for wētā

The wētā is a terrifyingly large insect of the grasshopper family with spiny hind legs, native to New Zealand. An adult wētā weighs around 70g. Weta is also the name of the creative workshop based in Wellington that made the models and designed the special effects in many of Peter Jackson's movie masterpieces, such as *The Hobbit* and *The Lord of the Rings*.

X is for *Xena, Warrior Princess*

Xena, Warrior Princess was a 1990s American TV series set in ancient Greece but filmed in New Zealand. It eventually aired in 108 countries around the world. Xena was played by Kiwi actress Lucy Lawless. The ambiguous nature of Xena's relationship with her sidekick Gabrielle led to Xena becoming a cult icon in the lesbian community worldwide.

Y is for 'Yeah, nah'

A brilliantly succinct, soothingly noncommittal and classically Kiwi way of saying that you have heard what another person has said, and you might agree – but then again you might not. 'People don't think much of the All Blacks' chances against South Africa this weekend...' 'Yeah, nah, she'll be right.'

Z is for zorb

The zorb is a large transparent sphere with another slightly smaller one inside it. You climb into the inner sphere and roll down a slope at great speed. The layer of air between the two spheres is supposed to protect you from injury as you spin down the slope. Invented by a New Zealander, naturally.

LOCAL KNOWLEDGE

Spoiled for choice: two national anthems

On 21 November 1977, the Government announced that the Queen had approved 'God Defend New Zealand' having equal status with 'God Save the Queen' as the national anthem of New Zealand. Whenever the national identity of New Zealand is to be emphasised, 'God Defend New Zealand' does nicely. If the Queen, other members of the royal family or the governor-general are present, we express loyalty to the Crown by singing 'God Save the Queen'. That is how we have ended up with two national anthems. 'God Defend New Zealand' has two verses, each in English and Māori. (The Māori version is not a direct translation of the English version.)

All together, let's stand and sing . . .

AOTEAROA   GOD DEFEND NEW ZEALAND

E Ihowā Atua   God of Nations, at Thy feet

O ngā iwi mātou rā   In the bonds of love we meet,

Āta whakarongona,   Hear our voices, we entreat,

Me aroha noa.   God defend our free land.

Kia hua ko te pai;   Guard Pacific's triple star

Kia tau tō atawhai   From the shafts of strife and war,

Manaakitia mai   Make her praises heard afar,

Aotearoa   God defend New Zealand.

RESOURCES AND ESSENTIAL READING

Bardsley, Dianne. *Book of New Zealand Words* (Wellington: Te Papa Press, 2013).

de Pont, Doris (ed). *Black: History of Black in Fashion, Society and Culture in New Zealand* (Auckland: Penguin, 2012).

Gardiner, Wira. *Haka: A living tradition*, 2nd edn. (Auckland: Hodder Moa, 2007).

Gordon, Elizabeth. *Living Language: Exploring Kiwitalk* (Christchurch: Canterbury University Press, 2010).

Hay, Jennifer et al. *Dialects of English: New Zealand English* (Edinburgh: Edinburgh University Press, 2008).

Hepözden, Rosemary. *The Daily Male: A Kiwi bloke's book of days* (Auckland: New Holland, 2013).

Hutchins, Graham. *Strictly Kiwi* (Auckland: Hodder Moa, 2010).

Ihaka, Kingi M, illustrated by Dick Frizzell. *A Pukeko in a Ponga Tree* (Auckland: Puffin, 2011).

Leach, Helen. *The Pavlova Story: A slice of New Zealand's culinary history* (Dunedin: Otago University Press, 2008).

Macalister, John, ed. *A Dictionary of Maori Words in New Zealand English* (Melbourne: Oxford University Press, 2005). Note that long vowels are not marked with macrons in the title or the content of this dictionary, because these words are now considered New Zealand English.

Oliver, Penny & Ian Batchelor. *Beach Bach Boat Barbecue: The complete collection* (Auckland: New Holland, 2013).

Orsman, H.W. *The Dictionary of New Zealand English* (Melbourne: Oxford University Press, 1997).

Romanos, Joseph. *New Zealand's Top 100 History-makers* (Wellington: Trio Books, 2005. Rev. edn, 2012).

Theobald, Nick & Pāora Walker. *Instant! Māori* (Wellington, Writer & Writer, 2004).

Tauroa, Hiwi & Pat. *Te Marae: A guide to customs & protocol* (Auckland: Reed Methuen, 1986).

Wolfe, Richard. *Kiwi: More than a bird* (Auckland: Random Century, 1991).

Websites

www.korero.maori.nz – in the Resources section, you can click on a map of New Zealand and hear how Māori placenames are pronounced

www.kupu.maori.nz/ – you can register to receive a Māori word a day, sent to your email or cellphone

www.maoridictionary.co.nz – a free online Māori–English dictionary

www.nzhistory.net.nz – provides a list of 100 Māori words that all New Zealanders should know, and you can listen to the words to find out how they are pronounced

www.stats.govt.nz – New Zealand's national statistical office

INDEX